Dollars and Diplomacy

The Impact of U.S. Economic Initiatives on Arab–Israeli Negotiations

Patrick L. Clawson
and Zoe Danon Gedal

Policy Paper N

D1306967

THE WASHINGTON INSTITUTE FOR NEAR EAST POLICY

Published in 1999 in the United States of America by the Washington Institute for Near East Policy, 1828 L Street NW, Suite 1050, Washington, DC 20036.

Library of Congress Cataloging-in-Publication Data

Clawson, Patrick, 1951–
  Dollars and diplomacy : the impact of U.S. economic initiatives on
Arab–Israeli negotiations / Patrick L. Clawson and Zoe Danon Gedal.
    p. cm. — (Policy paper ; no. 49)
  ISBN 0-944029-29-9 (pbk.)
  1. United States—Foreign economic relations—Middle East. 2. Middle
East—Foreign economic relations—United States. 3. Arab cooperation.
4. Middle East—Economic integration. 5. Economic assistance, American—Middle East. 6. Arab–Israeli conflict—1993– —Peace. 7. Peace—
Economic aspects—Israel. 8. Peace—Economic aspects—Palestine.
I. Gedal, Zoe Danon, 1965– . II. Washington Institute for Near East Policy.
III. Title. IV. Title: Impact of U.S. economic initiatives on Arab–Israeli
negotiations. V. Title: Impact of U.S. economic initiatives on Arab–Israeli
negotiations. VI. Series: Policy papers (Washington Institute for Near East
Policy); no. 49.
HF1455.Z4M6283 1999
337.73056—dc21   99-11811
                  CIP

Cover design by Monica Neal Hertzman. Cover photo © CORBIS/Wally
McNamee.

About the Authors

Dr. Patrick L. Clawson is director for research at The Washington Institute for Near East Policy. He is the editor most recently of *Iraq Strategy Review: Options for U.S. Policy*, and a coauthor of *Iran Under Khatami: A Political, Economic, and Military Assessment* (both Washington Institute, 1998). Dr. Clawson has also authored more than thirty scholarly articles on the Middle East, which appeared in *Foreign Affairs, International Economy, Oxford Bulletin of Economics and Statistics* and *Middle East Journal*, among other journals. He has written op-ed articles in the *New York Times, Wall Street Journal*, and *Washington Post*, among other newpapers. He has testified before congressional committees more than a dozen times. Dr. Clawson was previously a senior research professor at the Institute for National Strategic Studies of the National Defense University in Washington, D.C., where he was the editor of the Institute's flagship annual publication, *Strategic Assessment*, and before that. he was a research economist at the International Monetary Fund, the World Bank, and the Foreign Policy Research Institute. Dr. Clawson graduated with a Ph.D. from the New School for Social Research and a B.A. from Oberlin College.

Dr. Zoe Danon Gedal is a Soref research fellow at the Washington Institute for Near East Policy. She received her doctorate from the politics department at Brandeis University. Her primary field of study was international relations, with particular focus on domestic determinants of foreign policy and the role of non-state actors in global politics. She has spent several extended periods of time in Israel and the West Bank, and conducted research in Jordan and Egypt. Dr. Danon Gedal has lectured widely on various aspects of American foreign policy toward the Middle East and has written opinion articles for several newspapers. Prior to coming to the Washington Institute, Dr. Danon Gedal served as the policy director of the McGreevey gubernatorial campaign in New Jersey, and before that she served as deputy campaign manager of the Lerner congressional campaign in the Seventh District of New Jersey.

• • •

Contents

Acknowledgments

The authors are indebted to a great number of people who have been helpful in the formulation and preparation of this study. We are grateful to the more than fifty government officials, business leaders, and distinguished scholars who met with us in Egypt, Jordan, Israel, and the Palestinian areas, as well as the several dozen current and former officials whom we interviewed in Washington. Many did not want their comments attributed, and for that reason, we thought it would be more discreet not to list any of the interviewees.

The interviews were particularly important in this work, because the nature of the topic made statistical data of much less use than they would be in a purely economic work. The question we were exploring—the effect of U.S. economic initiatives on the peace process—made precise measurements impossible. Indeed, our topic makes rigorous analysis difficult, because there is no clear way to determine scientifically how much of an impact any given initiative or policy had on either high diplomacy (that is, the negotiation of diplomatic accords) or the normalization of relations among peoples. By the very nature of the question we are examining, we have had to rely on judgments. We realize that the best informed analysts and participants can reasonably differ in their interpretation of these matters.

This study was funded in part with a generous contribution from the CRB Foundation, which has taken the lead in promoting innovative ways to bolster the peace process through economics. Our gratitude also goes to the Samuel M. Soref and Helene K. Soref Foundation, supported the project through funding the research of Dr. Gedal. The Peres Center for Peace and the Center for Palestine Research and Studies were also instrumental in assistance with the research in the region. We are indebted to them and to the many people—including Dalia Dassa-Kaye, M. Graeme Bannerman, and Dov Zakheim—who helped us to sharpen our ideas and our writing by reading and commenting on earlier drafts. The insights we owe to those who helped us; the shortcomings are our own.

At The Washington Institute, we thank Robert Satloff and the rest of our colleagues who were both generous with their time and tolerant of our occasional lapses in charm throughout this project. We benefitted from the capable assistance of Chris Hoaldridge, Assaf Moghadam, Ben Orbach,

Stephanie Sines, Heiko Stoiber, and the rest of the research staff. Publications director Monica Neal Hertzman and her assistant Elyse Aronson have improved the manuscript immeasurably with their editorial expertise and patience. Zoe Danon Gedal thanks her husband, Samuel, for his unflagging encouragement, support, and enthusiasm.

Preface

The United States spends a great deal of time and money on economic efforts in the Levant, with the hope that these initiatives will promote progress in the peace process. Despite having primarily political goals, however, Washington tends to use economic indicators to evaluate the success of its Middle East initiatives. As the peace process and U.S. efforts to foster it will continue for the foreseeable future, The Washington Institute recognized the need to evaluate these economic programs based on the diplomatic goals that motivate them.

To address this topic, Patrick Clawson, our research director, and Zoe Danon Gedal, a Soref research fellow, analyze the relationship between economics and Middle East peace, highlight specific U.S. and regional initiatives, and include suggestions about what has been particularly helpful. Looking at ongoing and future programs, they comment on practices that could be improved and provide some general principles by which to plan and manage these initiatives.

In considering how aid can best help to cement support for peace treaties, Drs. Clawson and Gedal focus in particular on the difficult question of how to aid the West Bank and Gaza—specifically, how to support the Palestinian Authority (PA). They argue that the answer rests on how to balance the goals of promoting peace and advancing democractic economic development—that is, to what extent the United States should use its leverage from aid to press the PA to live up to its commitments to fight anti-Israel terrorism as well as to improve governance for the Palestinian people. A climate of political stability is the best inducement to private investment.

U.S. economic efforts to promote trade and investment can enhance people-to-people ties, but if oversold, they have the potential to damage the peace process by creating unfulfilled expectations. The authors note the success of behind-the-scenes, expert-level interaction in avoiding these problems and suggest greater efforts to depoliticize Middle East business interactions. One of the main conclusions of the study, in fact, is that if we want business to buttress politics, we have to take the politics out of business—that is, trade and investment cooperation should be based on sound business principles as well as on political motivations.

The Arab–Israeli peace process remains not only one of the highest priorities of U.S. foreign policy but also one of the most persistent challenges. We hope that this study will offer a new way of thinking about the role economic initiatives can play in achieving peace in this vital area of the world.

Mike Stein
President

Barbi Weinberg
Chairman

Executive Summary

The United States devotes considerable effort—more than $5 billion a year in aid, as well as many hours urging senior Arab and European officials to attend high-level meetings—to promoting the twin goals of economic prosperity and economic cooperation among states and peoples in the Levant. U.S. officials often speak of the two goals in one breath, implicitly advocating the idea that Arab–Israeli economic cooperation promotes prosperity and that prosperity in turn makes economic cooperation more attractive. Also, many Americans act as if it were obvious that these goals not only are worthwhile in and of themselves but also are ways to promote peace. The unstated assumptions seem to be, first, that prosperous people are happier and more confident and therefore more willing to make politically painful decisions and, second, that economic cooperation facilitates and may even catalyze political cooperation.

U.S. officials sometimes act as if initiatives for prosperity and cooperation can be worked out even when political disagreements exist, because doing business together serves everyone's self-interest. Yet, many in the Levant firmly believe that economics is a zero-sum game: If the other side is more prosperous, it will be a more powerful opponent rather than a more likely peace partner. At the popular level, a widespread attitude still exists that what is good for Arabs is bad for Israelis, and vice-versa. Furthermore, not everyone in the Middle East is convinced of the benefits of international economic cooperation with *anyone*, much less with former enemies. The forces of old-fashioned protectionism and narrow economic nationalism are powerful everywhere in the Levant, in Israel as well as in Arab states. Syrian president Hafiz al-Asad and many other Arabs seem to see economic integration—what former Israeli prime minister Shimon Peres called the "New Middle East"—as a plot for Israel to dominate Arab economies. To play on Peres's phrase, Asad fears banks as much as tanks.

The main conclusion of this study is that a sense of proportion is in order about what economics can do in support of Arab–Israeli peacemaking. In the Middle East, politics does come before business, but business can help to reinforce politics. Whereas economic efforts can be useful in supporting and cementing progress toward peace, they will rarely constitute enough of a force to pave a path from hostility to peace. At the same time, economic efforts can be a valuable aspect of peace facilitation within the realistic parameters of their potential: They can spread peaceful contact from the level of leaders to that of the people; they can create constituencies with a vested interest in peace; and they can promote prosperity that makes people more content with all aspects of their situation, even with a peace agreement they may otherwise find dubious.

That said, for most countries in the Levant, regional cooperation is not particularly important for their overall economic future. Israelis may see the market they offer as enormous relative to other regional markets, but Egyptian executives and officials point out that Israel's economy is not even 2 percent the size of the European Union (EU) market, which is where Egypt sells 40 percent of its exports. Similarly, the market of all the Arab states together is only about the size of the Dutch economy. Therefore, it is unrealistic to expect the opening of the Arab market to Israeli products to make a tremendous difference to Israel. Moreover, Arab states frequently erect barriers to trading with many of their neighbors, not just with Israel.

The one enormous exception to the rule that cooperation does not matter to the economies of the players is the Palestinian economy. Its prospects are greatly affected by the character of economic links with Israel. Economic cooperation between Israelis and Palestinians is recognized now by both sides as both necessary and inevitable, irrespective of what is happening on the political front. Yet, the two sides disagree on the merits of economic cooperation between Israel and other Arabs. The United States and Israel have promoted cooperation in part to advance normalization; Arab states have resisted cooperation in large part to avoid normalization. But if one agrees with this study's premise—that economic cooperation is useful for promoting prosperity and creating people-to-people contact regardless of politics—then economic cooperation is desirable irrespective of normalization. It is therefore sometimes desirable to separate business cooperation from normalization by emphasizing that economic cooperation takes place among individuals, not among countries.

This study examines three major kinds of U.S. economic initiatives and how effective they are in advancing peacemaking. The first is foreign aid earmarked for specific countries; this has primarily been given to promote prosperity in individual nations rather than cooperation among them. The other two initiatives are regionwide—economic summits and programs to promote trade and investment—both of which are designed to advance cooperation among Israelis and Arabs at least as much as to promote prosperity.

ECONOMIC AID

The predominant reason for U.S. economic aid to the region is political support for Israel, as opposed to support for the peace process. That support for Israel has several origins, from shared values to domestic U.S. political factors and common strategic interests—Israel was on the front lines during the Cold War facing Soviet clients with the latest Soviet-bloc arms. The United States shares strategic interests with others in the region as well; for example, Egypt is a politically important ally for Persian Gulf Security. But aid has also played a role in promoting peace; for instance, an economically and militarily stronger Israel has felt more comfortable taking the risks involved in the peace process.

Aside from using aid to cement peace agreements already reached, aid could in theory be used as a tool to pressure recipients into adopting more accommodating positions on the peace process. Such an effort was made during the Israel loan guarantee dispute of 1991–1992. It can be argued that U.S. pressure worked—that the pressure contributed to election results in Israel that led to a change in Israel's position toward settlements and toward the entire Madrid process—but only at a high price. However the loan guarantee episode is evaluated, the circumstances that allowed the United States to use aid as leverage in that case are unlikely to be repeated in the near future: It is implausible that recipients would agree to make significant changes on issues they feel are inimical to their security or national interests simply to sustain U.S. aid.

Israel. The absence of additional U.S. aid after the peace treaty with Jordan and the signing of the Oslo Accords seems to have had little if any impact on Israeli attitudes toward those agreements. One reason is those agreements did not lead to any substantial transition costs, unlike Camp David, which required extra security expenditures—such as for new and better airfields—to offset the security Israel lost by handing back the Sinai, a large buffer that separated Israel's heartland from Egypt. As Israel pulls back from additional areas in the West Bank, it will need to spend money to replace training camps and arms depots and to build roads to provide security for settlers. Additionally, Israel will feel more secure if it is able to modernize its antiterrorism equipment, from spy planes to attack helicopters. For these reasons, Israeli attitudes toward the Wye River agreement may be affected to a certain degree by the fact that the United States announced after the agreement a one-time $1.2 billion aid package proposed for 1999 to offset that agreement's costs. Even if U.S. aid makes only a small difference in the Israeli debate about redeployments and final status, if it is sufficient to tip

xiii

the scales that might otherwise be in balance between two opposing camps, it could be argued that a small difference is worthwhile.

Egypt. The basic rationale for supporting Egypt and strengthening the strategic partnership remains unchanged—to cement Egypt–Israel peace, the cornerstone of all peacemaking efforts; to assist the Egyptian regime in its battle against religious extremism for the hearts and minds of the Egyptian people; and to secure Egypt as a positive model of a pro-West, pro-peace, stability-promoting power for the states and peoples of the Arab and Islamic worlds. Yet, given the current degree of prosperity in Egypt and Egyptians' confidence about their economic circumstances, it may be possible to refashion the economic assistance program in such a way as to save money and at the same time invigorate the economic reform process. The principles that would govern such an economic aid package would be to phase out new commitments for projects, sustain the commodity import program (CIP), give priority to cash transfers, and complement the reduced aid with a program to enhance Egyptian exports.

U.S. military aid to Egypt has had some positive and some negative effects on the peace process. On the one hand, Egypt's strict implementation of the military aspects of the peace treaty with Israel, along with its record of operational support for U.S. initiatives, make a strong case that aid has made the Egyptian military more accepting of peace and more willing to work with the United States. On the other hand, the aid has signaled Washington's support for Egypt on broad strategic grounds irrespective of differences on the peace process. The current "cold peace" feeds the fear of many pro-Israel policymakers that the U.S.-funded modernization of Egypt's armed forces may create a threat to Israel's security. Yet, a number of safeguards remain firmly in place, not least the heavy dependence of the Egyptian military on U.S. logistical support. Moreover, there are a variety of reasons to sustain military aid to Egypt even if such aid has little positive impact on the peace process. In particular, military aid to Egypt is part of the U.S. strategy for the region—that is, Egyptian forces could be politically essential for demonstrating Arab support for any U.S.-led operation in the Persian Gulf.

Palestinians. Aid to Palestinians has been one of the most controversial parts of the U.S. assistance program. One issue has been the complaints from Palestinian Authority (PA) officials about miserly aid flows from all donors. In fact, the PA has received large sums of aid. A 1993 World Bank report estimated the Palestinian areas needed $1.44 billion in aid committed during 1994–1998. By contrast, the actual level of funds committed through June 1998, according to PA data, was $3.5 billion, of which $2.5 billion had been disbursed, most of it from European donors. The 1997 aid disbursed in the West Bank and Gaza, $545 million, was $203 per person and was the equivalent of 15 percent of GNP. By comparison, all international aid to India was $2 per person, or 0.6 percent of GNP. In other words, aid to the PA was well above what the World Bank had estimated would be needed and well above that received by much poorer countries. Indeed, reports by donors suggest that economic development was constrained much more by the political situation, such as the inefficiencies of Palestinian institutions and the frequent security closures imposed by Israel. Given that the aid to the Palestinians has been quite substantial, why is there a widespread impression among Palestinians that the donors have not lived up to their responsibilities? The answer is inflated expectations, the slow start of the aid program, and the political problems that have caused the economy to shrink despite generous aid.

In November 1998, the United States organized a conference dedicated to increasing aid to the Palestinians, at which the United States pledged a $400 million increase over five years, bringing total U.S. aid to $900 million for that period, compared to $500 million for the previous five years. But that conference focused on the wrong issue, namely, the size of the aid. More important is the issue of how the aid is used. To date, U.S. aid has been channeled through nongovernmental organizations (NGOs) or has been directly administered by the U.S. Agency for International Development (USAID) and has been destined for economic development, humanitarian relief, and democracy promotion. The question is whether this is the most effective way to promote the peace process. The implicit assumption underlying the current U.S. aid program is that the most important problems that can be breached with aid are poverty, suffering, and authoritarianism. These are not necessarily the key barriers to peace, however; it is worth considering if the aid program could address three other important obstacles to peace.

One important barrier has been the strength of the radical opposition in relation to that of Arafat and his mainstream political movement, Fatah. It is unclear if U.S. aid promoting fuller opportunities for the opposition to make itself heard alleviates or worsens this problem. Certainly the PA is an imperfect democracy, but it is by no means clear that those imperfections are the key barrier to peace—and it is worth bearing in mind that Arafat is a popular leader who might well receive majority support for strong presidential rule even in a perfect democracy. Under present circumstances, therefore, democracy promotion may not be the most important issue for the United States to support through aid.

A second major problem for the peace process has been the PA's lack of ability or of will to implement its obligations under the various peace accords. The PA argues that its institutional weakness has impeded its ability to take strong measures against violent peace process opponents. A different interpretation is that the PA leadership has been unwilling to make unpopular concessions to Israel that might attract the opposition of vocal pressure groups. Whatever the mix of inability and unwillingness, giving aid directly to the PA—as distinct from financing NGOs—could help. Such aid would allow the PA to carry out development projects much in the same way as ordinary governments use U.S. aid funds, and it would make the PA subject to all the same strict procedures to prevent fraud and to ensure that all funds are used for the purposes agreed to between PA and USAID. Allowing the PA to carry out projects on its own would help it to build institutional capabilities. It would also give the PA more political clout—through jobs and serviced provided—which could make the PA more willing to take politically difficult steps.

A third barrier to peace has been insufficient efforts to combat terrorism. Immediately after the 1993 Oslo Accords, Congress required that aid to the PA be contingent on determinations that the PA was fighting terrorism. That did not prove to be an effective means of encouraging more PA counterterrorism efforts; instead, it invited reports from the administration that certified compliance. A more effective approach would provide direct inducements—positive or negative—to the PA leadership to take specific steps to counter terrorism, which would make more concrete the commitments the PA has made in this regard. This will be hard to do and may not be possible, but it is worth exploring.

One possibility would be to use cash aid to the PA, with cash released when the PA has made specific, verifiable steps on counterterrorism. Such cash aid would provide Arafat the resources to create political support for his program, while leaving to the PA to decide how to accomplish this aim. In addition, this would free the PA from cumbersome and bureaucratic U.S. procedures. Some may argue that providing such cash aid is tantamount to financing PA corruption; however, the cash aid could be made contingent on satisfactory progress reported by the U.S. government on reducing fraud and corruption. The essential question that should govern whether to allocate cash aid to the PA is which would best serve the peace process: improving PA accounting standards and reducing corruption, or providing an incentive to fulfill peace—thus promoting objectives and helping to expand Arafat's political base so that he can afford to risk concessions to Israel.

Jordan. The U.S. aid program to Jordan since the peace treaty with Israel has not been the political success that the aid program to Egypt was after Camp David. The reasons for this are many. The Jordanian program started slowly, initially with debt relief that may have been important in the minds of Jordanian leaders but which did not directly affect the lives of ordinary citizens. Once expanded in 1997, the cash aid program was half the size of that in Egypt, relative to the size of the two countries: Comparing the average during the first five years of each, Egypt's was 7 percent of GNP and $70 per capita (in 1998 dollars) while Jordan's was 3 percent of GNP and $35 per capita. In addition, the Jordan aid program had to overcome a negative economic atmosphere when the high initial expectations for a post-peace economic boom were not realized. The 1998–1999 plan to increase aid to Jordan will bring the aid program for 1999 to $75 per capita, about the same aid per capita provided to Egypt after Camp David. Had the aid been at this higher level from the date of the Jordan–Israel peace treaty, the Jordanian attitude toward that treaty might have been much warmer.

The U.S. interest in a stronger Jordanian military would argue for military aid to Jordan irrespective of the peace process. Given the high reputation of the Jordanian military's training and readiness, upgrading Jordan's weaponry and logistical infrastructure may be one of the most effective ways to improve the readiness of a friendly Arab military to operate side-by-side with the United States during a regional crisis. U.S. military aid may also have reinforced the Jordanian military's willingness to work with Israel. Unlike the cold peace with Egypt, Israel's peace with Jordan involves extensive military-to-military contacts. All of this argues for expanding military aid to Jordan.

REGIONWIDE INITIATIVES

After the 1991 Madrid peace conference, and especially after the 1993 Oslo Declaration of Principles (DOP), much excitement was generated by regionwide initiatives, from multilateral peace talks to a series of economic summits that started in Casablanca. That enthusiasm is now gone. The main reason is that after the Israeli elections of 1996, Arab governments were more intent on withholding their own participation as a means of punishing Israel and the new Israeli government was concentrating its attention on issues like its new approach to bilateral talks rather than on regional economics. This dual development in attitudes left regionwide initiatives without any enthusiastic regional support during a period when bilateral negotiations were most in need of a boost. If these various multilateral efforts are to be reenergized, some lessons need to be drawn from the experience of 1991–1998.

The parts of the *multilateral peace talks* track that have continued to function are the expert-level meetings seeking pragmatic solutions to shared problems like water and the environment. These meetings fulfill many of the original goals of the multilaterals: They follow a functional approach that will, over time, contribute to building a constituency for peace; they involve a group of people from all sides who have working relationships with each other; and ultimately they provide a sense that the peace process can be helpful to citizens of the region in overcoming practical problems. By contrast, politically high-profile sessions have not functioned well. Part of the problem is that some Arab and European countries regard the multilateral talks primarily as a reward given by the Arab states to Israel for giving up land.

The first of the four annual *economic summits* was dominated by political jubilation, with the business atmosphere being secondary. As the years progressed, the close identification of the summits with the political peace process became a problem. The last two conferences, at Cairo and Doha, went forward only with a tremendous amount of U.S. persuasion. If the summits are to be revived, perhaps the most effective approach would be to give more emphasis to business rather than to governments. For instance, the U.S. delegation could be led by a prominent business executive like Bill Gates and supported by an undersecretary of commerce or state. That would advance the goal of fostering people-to-people contact while relegating political differences to the background.

The Middle East and North Africa Development Bank (MENABANK) initiative began with much promise, as it was the first initiative supported by the four core peace partners (Egypt, Israel, Jordan, and the PA), though many regarded the idea as only marginally useful from an economic perspective. The United States played a large role in encouraging the project and urging other states to support it; however, Washington delayed signing on and Congress resisted creating yet another regional development bank. Although the initial wisdom of promoting a bank can be debated, the failure to follow through on a U.S. initiative harmed U.S. credibility. The prospects for reviving the dormant MENABANK proposal are dim. The only hope would be to repackage it as a peace bank, rather than as a regional development bank.

TRADE AND INVESTMENT PROMOTION INITIATIVES

The United States granted a free trade agreement (FTA) to Israel in 1985, partly out of the conviction that a more prosperous Israel, with even more secure ties to the United States, would feel more confident in taking risks for peace. After the 1993 DOP, the United States became involved in a variety of initiatives to promote trade and investment, so as to make the Middle East more prosperous and to bring together Arabs and Israelis for mutual profit. Those initiatives have not cost much financially, nor have they yet had much economic impact. The initiatives have required a fair amount of time from government officials, but it could be argued that the political benefits merit the effort.

One initiative has been to provide privileged U.S. import status to projects run jointly by Israel and an Arab partner, such as industrial estates. The most successful project to date has been the Qualifying Industrial Zone (QIZ) in Irbid, Jordan. Starting industrial estates in the Palestinian territories has proved more difficult, although intensive U.S. efforts led to the inclusion in the Wye River Memorandum of a protocol for the long-delayed Gaza Industrial Estate, and that estate opened shortly thereafter, during Clinton's mid-December 1998 visit to Israel and Gaza.

International support for such joint projects would also help. The United States should further encourage the EU to support rather than continue to obstruct these estates, as obstructionism effectively closes the European market to products from these estates. Unlike the United States, the EU has preferred to continue to give trade privileges on a bilateral basis to individual Levant economies rather than to structure the privileges to encourage cooperation. Many in the Arab world prefer this approach of promoting prosperity, without much regard for cooperation between Arabs and Israelis; Egyptians in particular feel that their country is too important for its relations with the United States to be seen only through the lens of the peace process.

U.S. officials have also been involved in promoting trade among parties in the region by encouraging communication on trade policies and the reduction of nontariff barriers. The best prospects for success here seem to be unpublicized expert-level meetings, rather than the politically high-profile events that started what was known as the Taba Initiative among the region's commerce ministers.

As illustrated by the founding in 1993 of the group Builders for Peace, at that time there were high hopes that private sector investment funds from outside the region would increase prosperity and encourage the parties to work together. Top U.S. officials endorsed these efforts but then found there was little they could do to help. Moreover, U.S. officials did little to fulfill promises they had made with much publicity—for example, Overseas Private Investment Corporation (OPIC) insurance. One essential precondition for progress on efforts to attract private investment funds is to address the weak business climate in the PA-controlled areas, especially the widespread corruption by officials. Where corruption and insecurity are rampant, the prospects for private investment are dim.

A basic problem for regional trade is security. Trade can provide an oppurtunity for terrorists to smuggle bombs and weapons. Israeli security concerns thus lead to intensive, time-consuming examination of goods crossing the borders and, at times, the closures of those borders to people and goods. These border controls have done tremendous damage to the Palestinian economy. The United States has generally avoided questioning Israel's assessments of its security needs. Instead U.S. officials have sought to mitigate the damage by devising ways to minimize the economic effects of security-related restrictions.

U.S. officials have also tried to deal with the complications from Israelis who continue to favor protectionism and who believe that what is good for Arabs is bad for Israelis; such an attitude can lead to their using security as justification for protectionism and collective punishment. Some of the border restrictions have no apparent security rationale—for example, the insistence on Israeli inspections of exports from Gaza to Egypt or from the West Bank to Jordan, or the application of the closures to the pipeline bringing natural gas into Gaza.

Whereas U.S. efforts to mitigate border restrictions are time-consuming, frustrating, and often unrewarding from the point of view of improving the PA economy, the United States has gained much goodwill from Palestinian officials and executives. Observing the continuous U.S. efforts to facilitate border crossing has contributed to a Palestinian sense that the United States cares about them and is an honest broker, which has in turn increased the ability of the United States to facilitate peace process negotiations.

Final Warnings

Full economic cooperation among Israel, the PA, and Jordan—free trade, unfettered access for laborers, and welcoming attitudes toward foreign investment—would best promote prosperity. Yet, it may well be that Palestinians, for one, would be willing to pay a price in foregone income to achieve more autonomous economic institutions and less reliance on interaction with the Israeli economy. Therefore, it is not clear if full economic cooperation is best for the peace process.

Some economic initiatives can actually be destructive, as they create unfulfilled expectations that then embitter the populace. Part of the reason for these unmet expectations is people sometimes get the impression that an economic initiative will make a quick difference, when in fact most initiatives take years to become fully effective. Not only is it important to avoid making unrealistic forecasts, it is equally vital to make every effort to follow through on commitments once they are made. Especially when the diplomatic atmosphere is problematic, initiatives require sustained efforts and dedication at the highest levels. U.S. initiatives will be most effective if they are widely supported in Congress, and that support is usually easier to secure through early consultation between Congress and the executive branch. In other words, the main lesson of this study is aim low but be sure to deliver.

POLICY RECOMMENDATIONS

- Restart regionwide economic conferences, but put the focus on business, with leadership coming more from the private sector than from governments.

- Hold down popular expectations in the region about the economic effects that peace—and associated aid—will have in the short term. This can help to prevent the kind of disappointment that can undermine support for the peace process.

- Address economic problems on the most technical level possible. No issue in the Middle East is free from political overtones, and large plenary meetings can become hostage to grandstanding, which hardly advances people-to-people cooperation.

- Continue past 1999 aid to Jordan at the level per capita provided to Egypt after Camp David—that is, $70 per person (at 1998 prices).

- Prioritize objectives for the aid to the West Bank and Gaza, recognizing that one objective—securing fulfillment of Oslo and Wye commitments—is not always consistent with other objectives, like sustainable economic development and good governance (clean, transparent, and participatory).

- Allow the PA to carry out development projects with U.S. funding, rather than requiring that USAID or NGOs carry out such projects.

- Continue an active U.S. role in promoting trade and investment between Israel and its neighbors through low-publicity, expert-level, and private sector interactions; add to this a policy dialogue on overcoming protectionist and zero-sum attitudes.

- Repackage MENABANK as a peace bank rather than as a regional development bank, and fund it.

- Promote U.S. trade with and investment in Jordan, such as through extending to Jordan the free trade status given to Israel and the West Bank and Gaza, or through tax- or aid-financed incentives for investment.

Chapter 1

Economics and Politics

"The spirit of commerce, which is incompatible with war, sooner or later gains the upper hand in every state. As the power of money is perhaps the most dependable of all the powers (means) included under the state power, states see themselves forced, without any moral urge, to promote honorable peace and by mediation to prevent war wherever it threatens to break out."
—*Immanuel Kant,* Perpetual Peace

The United States devotes at least $5 billion a year in aid to the Levant, and U.S. policymakers have spent countless hours in the last five years coaxing senior Arab and European officials as well as private businesspeople to attend regional economic summits. The question asked in this study is, what effect does all this effort have on the peace process? What immediate impact on the Arab–Israeli peace negotiations resulted from the various U.S. government economic policy initiatives? Yet, this paper also looks at the indirect and long-term effects on the peace process, such as whether the economic initiatives create a better climate for consolidating peace.

In asking these questions, the authors consider three main kinds of initiatives:

- Foreign aid, by the United States and by others.
- Regionwide cooperation, including multilateral peace talks, economic summits, and the Bank for Economic Cooperation and Development in the Middle East and North Africa (MENABANK).
- Promotion of trade and investment between Arabs and Israelis, often including third-country partners, such as multinational corporations.

The authors evaluate the impact of regionwide cooperation, of trade and investment promotion, and of foreign aid on the peace process, not on the

1

economy. The two issues are quite distinct. For instance, it is possible that the economic summits, from Casablanca in 1994 to Doha in 1997, boosted investment in the region by multinational firms and put Arab businesspeople in touch with Israeli counterparts. Even so, these summits may not have had an appreciable effect on the positions and behavior of any of the parties to the diplomatic negotiations—business lobbies in the region may be too weak to influence governments, or Arab and Israeli businesspeople may take the attitude that the issues at stake in the peace process are too important for them to suggest changes for the mere pursuit of profit. Of course, in some cases economic policies may have been central to the peace process. For instance, concern among the Israeli electorate about the U.S. refusal to provide loan guarantees to Yitzhak Shamir's government may have been an important element in the election of Yitzhak Rabin, whose government proved to be more accommodating to peace process policies.

To judge economic policy initiatives by their impact on the peace process is arguably more appropriate than to judge them based on their economic impact. After all, it is quite plausible that economic policy initiatives were motivated more by the desire to promote the peace process than by the wish to help the region's economy. It hard to see Congress allocating large aid sums to Israel and Egypt solely for economic reasons: Even setting aside military aid, Egypt receives much more economic aid per capita than many other needy governments more actively engaged in market reforms, and Israel is by no means a poor country. Nor does it seem likely that high-level U.S. government officials would spend so much effort promoting attendance at Middle East economic summits solely out of concern for economic development; it seems much more plausible that an important motivation was to see Israel and Israelis accepted as part of the Middle Eastern scene.

This book's aim is to analyze ways to make economic policy initiatives more helpful for the diplomatic peace process. To that end, the authors will consider what aspects of those initiatives have been most important for the peace process and which have been least important. In doing so, the book will look not only at the effect of the economic policies that were adopted but also at what might have been the impact had a different set of economic policies been pursued. For instance, had the United States delivered large amounts of aid to the Palestinian Authority (PA)—aid on the scale of the post–Camp David assistance to Israel—would that have made a difference in the PA's stance on peace process issues, or for that matter on how far Israel felt it had to go to accommodate the PA if it was to preserve the close U.S.–Israel relationship?

It is difficult to judge the impact of economic cooperation initiatives because the outcomes—be they diplomatic or economic—depend largely on other factors. Almost always, a country's economic growth depends much more on the policies of the national government than on what the outside world does to assist that state. And of course, the fate of the peace process depends largely on noneconomic factors. The authors can therefore offer only qualitative judgments, based on their impressions, rather than any precise, quantitative measure of how great was the impact of the economic cooperation initiatives.

The focus here is on the actions of the U.S. government, not those of the broader international community. The authors discuss other states' economic policy initiatives, especially the large role of the European Union (EU) member countries, only to the extent that the U.S. government was involved in shaping such initiatives or that such initiatives were (or might be) significantly influenced by U.S. efforts. U.S. readers may not appreciate how important Europe is to the economy of the Levant, relative to the role played by the United States. In fact, for each of the core peace process economies (Israel, Egypt, Jordan, the Palestinian areas, Syria, and Lebanon), the United States is a smaller trading partner than is Europe. In some cases, the difference is striking. In 1997, the EU took 41 percent of Egypt's exports whereas the United States took 11 percent; for Syria, the comparable figures were 57 percent EU and 1 percent United States.[1] Even for Israel, which is more closely tied to the U.S. economy, the comparable figures were 30 percent EU and 19 percent United States.

Before turning to a consideration of the three families of U.S. economic policy initiatives—foreign aid, regionwide cooperation, and trade and investment promotion—a few words are in order about the relationship between economics and peace. Little consensus exists on how strong the tie is or in what ways it works. The authors' conclusion is that economics is a small factor in achieving peace but can be central to consolidating that peace, by demonstrating the advantages peace brings and by developing a network of people-to-people ties.

The main focus of this book is on what economics can do to help reach peace agreements and to consolidate those agreements while they are still in the early fragile years. Later chapters consider various ways that economics can contribute to those more short-term peace-promotion goals.

Chapters 2 and 3 discuss the role of foreign aid. Chapter 2 looks at the experience with the more recent entrants into the peace process: the PA, Jordan, Syria, and Lebanon. Chapter 3 examines the original peace partners, Israel and Egypt. A major issue in these chapters is whether substantial aid makes an important difference in either arriving at peace or in reinforcing peace once a treaty is signed. The evidence presented here suggests that, to some extent, more aid can mean higher economic growth, and a more prosperous people may be more content with life and therefore more willing to accept political compromises they might not particularly like.

Chapter 4 explores whether functional cooperation in areas of mutual economic advantage builds confidence. The evidence suggests cooperation does create interpersonal contacts but that it may not do as much to create political trust; indeed, when the political atmosphere sours, political suspicions often spill over into doubts about the motives of those seeking functional cooperation.

Finally, in terms of analysis, Chapter 5 considers the question of whether economics creates constituencies for peace—for instance, whether businesspeople profiting from peaceful economic interaction may form an informal caucus lobbying for more flexibility in the peace process. There are some limited signs that this happened in the short term. Yet, significant barriers exist to hinder such lobbying: Local populations and governing elites give more importance to politics than to economics; Middle East societies have limited experience with businessmen lobbying on such issues; and only Israel is a fully democratic country in which popular opinion ultimately determines government policy.

ECONOMICS AND PEACE

Vigorous disagreement occurs among analysts and policymakers about how closely peace and economics are connected. Common sense suggests that the causality works both ways: Peace is good for growth, and trade and prosperity are conducive to peace. Yet, these relationships are hard to demonstrate.

The effect of peace on economic growth is less than might be thought. In particular, the "peace dividend"—that is, lower military spending after attaining peace—may not matter much. A substantial body of literature demonstrates that military spending has a relatively small impact on economic growth. Yet, military spending has some positive spin-offs that offset most of the negative effects of diverting resources that could be spent on investment.[3] It is worth reflecting on the lack of any obvious correlation between countries that have low military spending and those with high growth, or between those with high military spending and those with low growth. For instance, sub-Saharan Africa has the lowest military spending, both absolutely and relative to national income, of any region, but it also has the lowest growth rate, while countries like South Korea and Taiwan have had high military spending as well as high growth.

Furthermore, it is not clear how soon after peace the Levant would enjoy a peace dividend. The immediate impact of peace for Israel may actually be an increase in military spending, as new facilities are built to make up for those in areas handed over to Arab peace partners. For instance, withdrawal from the Sinai after Camp David led Israel to spend billions of dollars (largely financed by the United States) to replace the military facilities, especially the two large air bases, that it relinquished. Were Israel to withdraw from the Golan Heights, it would have to construct new bases for armored units; if it were to give up access to its intelligence listening posts, it might have to rely instead on high-cost intelligence satellites or airplanes. Similarly, since the peace treaty with Israel, the Jordanian military has been hit with the heavy cost of redeploying to face the increased security threat from Iraq and Syria. In general, the signing of a peace agreement may not be sufficient to end the mutual mistrust, and therefore countries would continue to maintain large militaries equipped with modern weapons.

For the Levant, quite probably more important than the peace dividend is the effect of peace on the investment climate. When the Oslo accords and the Israeli–Jordanian Peace Treaty created the sense that the Arab–Israeli conflict was on the way to resolution, investors the world over became more interested in the region. In just three years (1995–1997), Israel alone received more than twice as much direct foreign investment as it received in the previous two decades (1975–1994)—that is, $6.1 billion compared to $2.8 billion.[4]

Peace also affects tourism, which is a significant source of foreign exchange for the region. Comparing 1992 (before Oslo) and 1995 (before the terror attacks hit hard), earnings from tourism rose sharply in Israel, Jordan, and Egypt. Conversely, when terrorists attack, the entire region suffers: The November 1997 slaughter of foreign tourists in Luxor, Egypt, was a major reason behind the 11 percent decline in tourist arrivals in Israel during the first half of 1998 (compared to the previous year), even though Israel itself suffered few terrorist attacks during 1997–1998.[5]

Despite a broad consensus that peace helps the economy (though more modestly than might be desired), no such consensus exists about whether the economy has as much of an effect on peace. Perhaps the most famous optimist about economics and peace was Immanuel Kant. In his book *Perpetual Peace*, a central argument is

> The spirit of commerce, which is incompatible with war, sooner or later gains the upper hand in every state. As the power of money is perhaps the most dependable of all the means included under state power, states see themselves forced, without any moral urge, to promote honorable peace and by mediation to prevent war whenever it threatens to break out.[2]

Modern political scientists are deeply divided in their understanding of what drives international relations, with the two main camps being "liberals" and "realists."[6] Liberals argue that interdependence promotes peace, by increasing the flow of ideas and cultural contacts and also by creating economic interests that benefit from peace.[7] Realists, on the other hand, argue that economic interdependence makes a country more vulnerable and more likely to lash out when it sees its vital supplies at risk.[8] Clearly, which view is correct makes quite a difference for evaluating whether promoting economic cooperation among Middle East countries will promote peace.

Surprisingly, few political scientists—liberal or realist—address whether prosperity makes war more or less likely. Perhaps one can extrapolate from the general principles of each view. Liberals often argue that poverty and unemployment are the breeding grounds for extremism and hatred, which suggests that poverty could make war more likely. On the other hand, realists emphasize conflicting national interest and power as a source of conflict, which would seem little affected by prosperity; indeed, a more prosperous country may be more powerful and therefore better placed to make war. Still others argue that ideological, nationalist, and ethnoreligious disputes lie at the heart of many wars, and that these disputes are at most marginally affected by economic circumstances. History offers no clear guidance on these matters. The "impoverishment causes war" theory looks attractive as an explanation for World War II, for example, whereas the "poverty is peripheral to war" view looks more persuasive regarding World War I.

It would seem that many of the ways in which economics contributes to peace are felt only in the long term—that is, not for at least a decade. Therefore, despite their current lack of influence, economic efforts may turn out to be more important than initially realized. Given that many of the economic initiatives considered here began in the last decade, the positive effects of those initiatives may only now be felt to any degree.

ECONOMICS AND THE APPROACH OF THE PLAYERS

The effect U.S. economic efforts have on the peace process depends on the attitude each of the regional players takes toward the interplay between economics and politics. If the countries involved see no connection between the two, or if they believe that economics must follow political change rather than pave the way for it, the potential effectiveness of any economic initiative is severely limited. Similarly, particular efforts can be most influential when they are planned and executed with the attitudes of the players taken into account.

The regional parties' positions can be usefully compared not only with each other, but also with the attitude that has guided U.S. policy. American officials have worked under the assumption that peace and prosperity reinforce each other. The logic of economics fostering peace was voiced by Secretary of Commerce William Daley when he accompanied President Bill Clinton in a visit to Israel and Gaza in December 1998. He argued in a speech before the Israel–America Chamber of Commerce that Israelis should reach out to Arabs economically, because economic cooperation would pay a dividend in terms of building a constituency for peace. He stated that more jobs and hope for Palestinians would make them less likely to "be on the streets making trouble."[9]

Daley also argued that, "As important as politics is to the region, without jobs and economic security, no peace will take hold."[10] Secretary of State Madeleine Albright drew an even stronger connection, remarking during a joint press conference with King Hussein of Jordan that "prosperity is a parent to peace, just as desperation feeds extremism and violence."[11]

Among regional parties, whose basic attitudes on the economic–peace connection are discussed below, much more focus is placed on the potential for peace to bring economic gain than for prosperity to foster peace. The major exception to this, a small segment of the Israeli polity that shares the American penchant for economic cooperation for the purpose of peace, is ignored by many in the region and seen by some others as frightening. Generally speaking, Americans promote prosperity in the hopes that it will bring peace, while Middle Easterners seek peace in the hopes that it will bring prosperity.

The Palestinian Authority

In several significant respects, the relationship between peace and economics is different for the Palestinians than for any other party. Although others can debate the extent to which peace and normalization may enhance their economic opportunities, the Palestinians are in a situation in which the peace process is the *central* aspect of their economy. The combination of foreign aid related to the peace process, close economic ties to Israel, and the uncertainty caused by their indeterminate status make the peace process the primary determinant of Palestinian economics.

For Palestinian Authority chairman Yasir Arafat and most other prominent Palestinian leaders, all considerations take a back seat to politics, and
this has led to some frustration for ordinary Palestinians coping with dire
economic circumstances. In an opinion poll taken in April 1997, a plural-
ity of respondents (39.8 percent) considered the need to improve the economic situation to be the single most important issue facing Palestinian
society. By contrast, 23.1 percent cited "completing negotiations with Israel," 11.8 percent named the advancement of democracy, and 10.9 percent said maintaining order and security.[12] Yet, Arafat has devoted many
more resources to his extensive security apparatus than to economic development; the precarious political situation both with the Israelis and in-
ternally leads him to focus on maintaining and cementing power. Economic
development is at best a secondary consideration, receiving the PA's attention primarily when it is seen as being politically advantageous.

Undoubtedly, Arafat started out on the road to Oslo hopeful that an improved standard of living in the wake of peace would generate approval for
the agreement among Palestinians who might otherwise be skeptical. The
prospect of economic improvement was held out to the Palestinian public as
a reason to support the Oslo accords. Khaled Abdel-Shafi, a Palestinian economist who serves on the Gaza city council, places great weight on the role of
economic expectations in winning public support for the deal:

> At first there was a lot of talk of Gaza becoming the Singapore of the
> Middle East. That's why, to a great extent, people supported the peace
> agreement, which in many ways is a bad deal for the Palestinians. They
> hoped at least the economic situation would improve.[13]

This hope has been dashed as the post-Oslo years have seen a decline in
economic conditions in the West Bank and even more so in Gaza. By all
accounts, unemployment has risen and the standard of living has declined
for Palestinians in the years since the Declaration of Principles was signed.
A fear exists not only among PA leaders but also among American officials that the economic crisis in the West Bank and even more so in Gaza
will have a detrimental effect on Palestinian attitudes toward the peace
process, and that it could threaten stability and security in Palestinian-
controlled areas. In June 1998, Under Secretary of State Stuart Eizenstat
warned an Israeli audience that the crisis in Palestinian incomes and hope
is causing a "risk of diminishing the constituency for peace, not only among
the public at large but increasingly among Palestinian businesspeople."[14]

Ironically, Arafat's focus on politics over economics, which stems from his tenuous political status, has actually caused political problems for the PA. The decision to use donor funds to strengthen the security forces as opposed to the infrastructure or social services is a prime example of this phenomenon. The Islamist opposition group Hamas has taken advantage of this gap to continue its pre-Oslo practice of providing a number of social services under its own auspices—meeting needs as basic as health care and child care—which thereby contributes to public support for the group.

The Palestinians would prefer other Arab states to avoid progress in economic interaction with Israel until further strides are made on the Israeli–Palestinian track. They see such economic relationships as weakening whatever Arab leverage exists. These attitudes frustrate some Israelis, who argue that the Arabs actually stand to gain more economically from cooperation than Israel does, and that increased ties make it politically easier for any Israeli government to make concessions in the peace process.

Israel

Israelis have divided opinions on the relationship between economics and politics. An oversimplified but instructive distinction among Israelis is between those who see Palestinian development and improved economies for their Arab neighbors as crucial for Israel's future, and those who continue to think of economic relations with the Arabs as a zero-sum game. The former group is frustrated by the latter, as are many Arabs.

Among those Israelis who see Palestinian economic development as beneficial to Israel, some stress the long-term probability that a prosperous neighbor will make a better neighbor. They believe a continued, dramatic difference in standards of living between Israel and its neighbors will be an unending source of friction. Some Israelis seen as unsympathetic to Palestinians nevertheless believe that, in an immediate sense, poverty serves as fodder for the extremism that threatens Israeli security. This is a belief that U.S. officials tend to agree with and encourage. Under Secretary Eizenstat specifically urged this view during a news briefing in Tel Aviv: "Israel needs to define security in a broader sense. A prosperous neighbor is in Israel's security interest. If the economic hopes of Israel's neighbors are dashed, this hurts security."[16]

Despite allegations by some Israelis interviewed, there is a fierce debate in Israel about how to achieve security while alleviating Palestinian suffering. Although some remain convinced that Israeli security is best served by blocking Palestinians from entering Israel at sensitive times, others argue that the loss in income caused by closures contributes to the despair that pushes Palestinians into the arms of Hamas and the Palestinian Islamic Jihad.[17]

In addition to the general benefits of normalizing with neighbors and the particular concerns about poverty feeding Palestinian extremism, many Israelis recognize that they do gain economically from the peace process. Whereas most Israelis agree that regional markets do not provide particularly lucrative prospects for Israeli exporters, they realize that the peace process increased foreign investment from outside the region. International corporations that had shied away because of the Arab boycott and general regional instability began investing in Israel in much greater numbers after Oslo.

Even some of the most security-minded Israelis are concerned with the economic health of their Arab neighbors. During a visit to the United States in December 1998, Foreign Minister Ariel Sharon, the same minister who was delivering a tough line on conditions for implementing the Wye Memorandum, urged Jewish Americans to look out for the Jordanian economy as part of their work in behalf of Israeli security. In a meeting with the American Jewish Committee, he suggested that they organize trips for businesspeople to visit Jordan.[15] This is a completely separate goal from normalization, as it promotes investment in Jordan without stipulating any type of direct Israeli involvement. Similarly, most Israeli officials interviewed would like to see enhanced economic cooperation with their neighbors grow regardless of the status of political negotiations at any given moment.

Along with Israelis who are *indifferent* to the prospect of economic normalization in the region, some Israelis who are *opposed* to increased economic ties with their Arab neighbors are motivated by political fears and specific financial interests. Top Israeli economic officials explain that many low-level bureaucrats who work at border crossings are stuck in an outdated belief that causing trouble to Arabs in any way is a form of service to Israel. Yet, a more important force behind Israeli reluctance for economic interaction with Arabs is concern about jobs lost. Those Israelis hardest hit by unemployment, and those segments of the society left behind by the technological revolution, view the cheaper Arab labor markets as competitors for jobs. Some Israeli officials interviewed describe a process of constant struggle to make the bureaucrats working at the borders more accommodating to Palestinians and to convince other Israelis that helping the Palestinian economy is in Israel's interest.

Proponents of economic integration tend to see it as a valuable political as well as economic end. This was certainly more true for the previous

Labor government—famous for then–Prime Minister Shimon Peres's ideas of a "New Middle East"—than it is for the current Likud-led coalition. Yet, some Israelis—including Labor supporters and businesspeople—as well as Arabs fault the Labor government's enthusiasm for having encouraged Arab populations to harbor unrealistic hopes that the peace process would bring immediate and dramatic financial rewards. They also blame it for engendering suspicion among their Arab partners regarding the possibility of ulterior Israeli motives. Labor's willingness to move toward political separation between the West Bank and Gaza and Israel may also have (ironically) resulted in policies that hurt the Palestinians economically in the short term.

Just as economic attitudes toward the peace process do not necessarily indicate Israelis' political attitudes, their political attitudes are not a completely reliable predictor of their approach toward economic policies that affect the Palestinians. A number of Israeli and Arab leaders have observed that, although the Labor government offered a much better political atmosphere in which to attempt business, the Likud government has been at least as forthcoming with specific economic measures. Prime Minister Netanyahu has reported proudly on improvements in the Palestinian economy and increases in the number of Palestinians working in Israel, citing a relaxation of some of the restrictions on Palestinian laborers.[18] He has noted his frustration with what he describes as a "tremendous gap of perception" between the facts of his government's economic policy toward the Palestinians and the widespread view that Israel is stifling the Palestinian economy.[19] Netanyahu has gone as far as to claim that "there has never been a more liberal, more conciliatory, more open, more generous treatment of the Palestinian economy than under this government."[20] In contrast to Peres, Netanyahu is motivated by a desire to avoid full separation and blur the "green line"—a desire that results in certain short-term economic benefits for the Palestinians.

Israeli leaders who favor economic normalization with their neighbors greatly appreciate America's role. Several high-level officials in the Israeli finance and foreign ministries interviewed noted that enthusiasm for particular peace projects, when coming from U.S. officials, reduces the suspicion from Arabs that the projects are plots for Israeli domination of the regional economy.

Jordan

Jordan had been the Arab government most amenable to a warm peace with Israel, and an openness to economic normalization has been an element of that. For Jordan, geopolitical realities, particularly in the wake of the Gulf War, present limited opportunities for economic development, and some Jordanian leaders and analysts view peace primarily as a means to improve the regional standard of living. This economic focus has become increasingly central as Jordanian financial conditions have worsened and the threat of social unrest and instability has grown. The failing health of King Hussein, given that the majority of Jordanians have never known life under any other ruler, has further contributed to a sense of uncertainty.

Jordanian government leaders gripe about specific Israeli economic policies, but they generally accept the idea of doing business with Israel. They recognize, though, that a fundamental opposition to normalization is widespread and growing among the population. A poll of Jordanian university students taken in December 1998, for example, showed that 87.7 percent of the respondents opposed normalization with Israel. The same poll indicated that 64 percent believe Jordan's economic situation deteriorated after the peace treaty with Israel.[21] Officials worry about the ability of the government to continue on the current course in the absence of political progress to diffuse public anger. Domestic problems are exacerbated by sharp and often public criticism directed at Jordan from other Arab governments and commentators, because of the kingdom's willingness to cooperate with Israel absent a comprehensive peace agreement.

The Jordanian government realizes it has received certain economic benefits from its accommodating approach in the peace process. Debt forgiveness, economic aid, and the Qualified Industrial Zone agreement have all accrued to Jordan primarily because of the peace process. Despite a small amount of grumbling about the low level of aid compared to that received by Israel and Egypt, leaders recognize that the country has benefited from peace with Israel. Yet, some officials say the economic efforts have had a smaller impact than most Jordanians expected. Jordanian leaders do not tend to blame U.S. officials for the popular frustration and disappointment. They generally place the blame for unrealistic expectations on their own government, which used the possibility of financial gain to decrease opposition to the peace agreement with Israel and its then–Labor government.

In addition to the frustration caused by unmet expectations for a peace dividend, much of the Jordanian public is also concerned that Israel is plotting to take over the Jordanian economy and purchase control of Jordanian companies. Jordanian leaders interviewed found this ironic, as Israelis have hardly rushed to invest in the Jordanian economy despite having every opportunity. Yet, the leadership's inability to reassure the public about this is indicative of the level of mistrust that prevails. It is also emblematic of the striking divisions between the Jordanian government and much of the public on matters relating to Israel. Unfortunately, most business elites and professional associations have stood in opposition to the government, on the side of antinormalization public sentiment. Opposition political parties have also come out unequivocally against normalized economic and political ties: A statement issued by all thirteen opposition parties in March 1998 complained about the government "rapidly normalizing ties with the 'Zionist enemy,' despite the hostile Israeli stance toward the Arab nation."[22]

Despite these public doubts and resentments, Jordanian leaders interviewed took a generally positive view toward U.S. economic initiatives. Like the Palestinians and Egyptians, however, most Jordanians interviewed urged the U.S. government to focus more of its efforts on encouraging the political process between the PA and Israel. They argued that an improved political climate would make economic possibilities much more viable.

Egypt

Egyptians interviewed for this research were generally united in the viewpoint that, in the peace process, economics cannot precede politics. The only real division is between some who are convinced that, ideally, economic developments and political progress should occur simultaneously, and the majority who say economic normalization can come only after political problems are solved. The thinking behind this is that normalization is a "favor" to Israel. Like many other Arabs, many Egyptians suspect Israel of trying to circumvent Palestinian rights and aspirations by building relationships with the surrounding Arab states. Perhaps lingering sensitivity about playing into that perceived Israeli scheme by signing the Camp David accords makes Egyptians especially wary of the type of cooperation Jordan is engaged in with Israel.

Egyptians interviewed saw Israel's perceived desire for normalization as largely political rather than purely economic. They see Israel's desire for normalization as providing Arabs with one of the few available items of leverage. Many Egyptians hope the Arabs can use the prospect of Israel's full acceptance into the region to pressure Israel to make concessions in the peace process. Similarly, they see the threat of reversing past Arab steps toward normalization as a means to elicit Israeli compliance. Whereas Palestinian opposition to normalization is based on a concern that their own political goals be met, Egyptians seem more concerned with domestic public opinion and their perceived status as leaders of the Arab world. They see themselves as the key actor in any pan-Arab ambition.

Many Egyptian politicians and businesspeople believe their best financial prospects lie outside the region. They are enthusiastic about their trade with European countries and are eager to increase trade with their largest single trading partner, the United States. Trade with these parties is in no way dependent on cooperation with Israel. Some are offended that many international companies use Israel as a regional base, a role that many Egyptians feel naturally belong to their country. There is no evidence that Egyptians see the possibility of business with Israel as enough of a draw to compromise their political principles.

Syria

Syria has made its position on economics and the peace process abundantly clear by refusing to participate in either the multilateral talks or any of the economic integration projects, even back in the halcyon days of the peace process. Syrian president Hafiz al-Asad's attitude is that Israel should not be integrated into the region until it meets the demands of all Arab states for the return of land, including his own requirement of full return of the Golan Heights. Syria has joined other rejectionist states in openly criticizing those Arab states that have participated in regionwide events like the MENA summits, and its hostility toward Jordan over this matter has been harsh and sustained.[23]

Syria's hostility toward economics as a means toward peace came out clearly when Shimon Peres was Israel's prime minister. Peres put Uri Savir in charge of Israel's negotiations with Syria, and Savir—like Peres, a great believer in peace-promoting potential of economic cooperation—arrived at the December 1995 meeting with suggestions for eighteen separate agreements to facilitate the transition to peace, from abrogation pf boycotts to the establishment of postal ties.[24] Syrian chief negotiator Walid Mua'allim insisted that cooperation was something that had to follow the termination of the state of war. Although he relented to the point that he was prepared to discuss many issues like diplomatic relations, he was adamant about economic relations: "He could not say at present, when a state of war obtained between the two countries, that Syria would establish bilateral economic relations with Israel."[25] He cited three reasons for Syrian trepidation: history and sensibilities, the gap between the level of development of the two economies, and Syrian fear of Israeli economic hegemony. Summarizing his experiences with the Syrian negotiators over the years, Israeli negotiator Itamar Rabinovich said Asad was more wary of Peres's creative ideas about economic ties than he had been of Rabin's tough, no-nonsense focus on security matters.[26]

An additional reason why Asad is reluctant to discuss economic cooperation is that he prefers a command-style economy, which gives the political authority tight control. Asad may feel threatened by any opening of Syria's economy—he does not trust private Syrian entrepreneurs, much less those who would trade with Israel.

POLICY ISSUES

U.S. efforts to foster advancements in the peace process through economic initiatives can succeed only to the extent that the parties are amenable to the connection. Clearly, not all of the parties are equally open to the relationship as envisioned by the Americans. Based on the prevailing attitudes of each regional party, the potential for initiatives to work is directly related to the political atmosphere. In the absence of political progress, regionwide economic initiatives do not hold much promise for political dividends. Yet, certain factors make it reasonable for U.S. officials to persevere in the face of these obstacles.

One possibility that may motivate American officials to push on in the face of regional resistance to the economics–peace connection is that long-term benefits may exceed immediate rewards. A number of U.S. officials at all levels have expressed the belief that economic prosperity and a lasting peace can only be achieved together. In the words of Under Secretary Eizenstat, "Peace and stability are intrinsically tied to jobs and prosperity."[27] This philosophy allows for a long-term sense of building a foundation upon which peace can be constructed when politics allows, which would invalidate the tendency to make purely immediate assessments of the success of these policies.

Some in the region are concerned that the economic initiatives may be viewed as a substitute for involvement in the political realm. In general, Palestinians and Egyptians, and to a lesser extent Jordanians, have some reservations about large, symbolic economic programs that are used to create an impression of peace in the region, as the prospect of actual peace seems further and further away. Whereas this falsely positive image may be useful in attracting outside investors to the region, many Arabs fear that it also reduces international pressure on Israel to continue with the peace process. Yet, Middle East policymakers and businesspeople interviewed about U.S. economic efforts almost universally agreed that these efforts cannot hurt. Leaders of the peace process countries see the attempts at mediating specific disputes as helpful, even when the efforts have only minimal impact. One prevalent theme voiced by those interviewed was that, as bad as things have gotten, they would be worse without American dedication.

NOTES

1   International Monetary Fund, *Direction of Trade Statistics 1998*, pp. 197–198, 274–275, and 264–265.

2   Immanuel Kant (Lewis Beck, ed.), *Perpetual Peace* (New York: The Liberal Arts Press, 1957), p. 32.

3   Todd Sandler and Keith Hartley, *The Economics of Defence* (Cambridge: Cambridge University Press, 1995), pp. 200–220. These pages review the extensive debate kicked off by two controversial 1970s articles by Emile Benoit which showed that countries with higher defense spending had higher growth rates.

4   Direct investment by non-residents as reported by Bank of Israel, *Annual Report 1997* (Jerusalem: Bank of Israel), 1998, p. 342.

5   Israel Central Bureau of Statistics, *Monthly Bulletin of Statistics*, November 1997, table E11, "Arrivals and Departures, by Type of Visa," from http://www.cbs.gov.il/.

6   The debate between liberalists and realists on economics and peace is reviewed in Dale Copeland, "Economic Interdependence and War," *International Security* 20, no. 4 (Spring 1996), pp. 5–41.

7   The classic statement is Norman Angell, *The Great Illusion,* 2nd edition (New York: G.P. Putnam's Sons, 1933). A similar modern theory is Richard Rosecrance, *The Rise of the Trading State* (New York: Basic Books, 1986). A theory that emphasizes "complex interdependence" including cultural and intellectual ties is Robert Keohane and Joseph Nye, *Power and Interdependence* (Boston: Little, Brown, 1977).

8   See the writings of Kenneth Waltz, such as "The Myth of National Interdependence," in Charles Kindleberger, ed., *The International Corporation* (Cambridge, Mass.: MIT Press, 1970), pp. 205–223; and Robert Gilpin, such as "Economic Interdependence and National Security in Historical Perspective," in Klaus Knorr and Frank Trager, eds., *Economic Issues and National Security* (Kansas City: Regents Press of Kansas, 1977), pp. 19–98.

9   "Remarks by U.S. Secretary of Commerce William M. Daley, Israel–American Chamber of Commerce," (Washington: Federal Document Clearing House, December 13, 1998).

10 Ibid.

11 "News Conference with King Hussein of Jordan and Secretary of State Madeleine Albright," in Amman, Jordan (Washington: Federal News Service, September 14, 1997).

12 Jerusalem Media and Communication Centre (JMCC), "Public Opinion Poll no. 19, On Palestinian Attitudes Towards Current Issues, April 1997," *JMCC Public Opinion Polls on Palestinian Attitudes Towards Politics, nos. 1–23, 1993–1997.*

13 Quoted in Lee Hockstader, "For Palestinian Residents of Gaza, Five Years of Peace Bear Bitter Fruit," *Washington Post*, September 14, 1998.

14 Ibid.

15 "Israel's Foreign Minister, AJC Leaders Discuss Peace Process Concerns," American Jewish Committee Press Release, December 7, 1998.

16 Quoted in David Makovsky, "U.S. Asks Israel to Help Improve Palestinian Standard of Living," *Ha'aretz* (English internet edition), June 16, 1998.

17 The debate is described by Haggai Huberman, "A Prolonged Closure is a Security Threat," *Hatzofeh* (in Hebrew), September 16, 1998.

18 "Economic Relations Between Israel and the Palestinian Authority," Israeli Government Press Office Press Release, May 25, 1998.

19 "Prime Minister Netanyahu Before the Foreign Diplomatic Corps," May 22, 1998, released by the Information Division of the Israeli Foreign Ministry.

20 Ibid. U.S. State Department officials are critical of the report for painting an overly rosy picture by citing facts selectively, and others fault it for making comparisons to the post-Oslo Labor government period instead of to pre-Oslo figures. From a confidential interview with State Department officials, June 5, 1998.

21 "Poll: 87.7% of University Students Against Israel," *al-Majd*, December 18, 1998, p. 12, in Foreign Broadcast Information Service, Near East and South Asia, FBIS-NES-98-362, December 28, 1998.

22 "Jordan: Opposition Concerned Over Public Freedoms, Foreign Presence," *Jordan Times* (internet edition), March 22, 1998.

23 Syria's "targeting" of Jordan because of its ties to Israel, and urging of Jordan to sever those links, are referred to in Alia A. Toukan, "Jordan Will Seek Arab Unity at Jerusalem Committee Meeting," *Jordan Times* (internet edition), July 27, 1998.

24 This paragraph draws heavily on Itamar Rabinovich, *The Brink of Peace* (Princeton, N.J.: Princeton University Press, 1998), pp. 200–225. Rabinovich provides a meeting-by-meeting account of the Syrian and Israeli positions as well as of U.S. activities.

25 Ibid., pp. 212–213.

26 Itamar Rabinovich in a talk given at the Washington Institute for Near East Policy, September 16, 1998.

27 Stuart Eizenstat, prepared statement before the House Committee on Appropriations, Subcommittee on Commerce, Justice, State, the Judiciary, and Related Agencies, May 8, 1996 (Washington: Federal News Service, May 8, 1996); later restated at speech to U.S. businesspeople in New York, October 2, 1996, promoting the Cairo MENA conference.

Chapter 2

Aid to Newer Peace Process Participants

U.S. aid to the peace process countries has differed greatly among the actors. Israeli–Egyptian peace led the United States to provide both countries with substantial financial assistance, whereas neither the Oslo accords nor the Israel–Jordan treaty prompted aid on anything close to the same scale. The obvious question to examine is whether the difference in aid flows has influenced the stability and depth of the peace processes between Israel and its three Arab partners. Because of the differences in aid flows and other circumstances surrounding the signing of peace treaties and accords, this chapter will focus specifically on the more recent entrants to the peace process—the Palestinian Authority, Jordan, Syria, and Lebanon. Chapter three will then look at Israel and Egypt, how post–Camp David aid facilitated peacemaking, and how that aid has been changing in recent years.

At first glance, it may seem peculiar to argue that cash from an outside power is needed to make peace desirable: Peace would seem to be its own reward. In addition, the usual argument is that peace brings an economic dividend, which would make it seem unnecessary to have a peace "bribe"—a cash payment to induce peacemaking. But, in fact, the Middle East peace agreements have been controversial domestically (the exception proving the rule being the universal support in Israel for the Jordan treaty). Moreover, many of the benefits of peace are obvious only over the long run, so the peace treaties may look problematic in their early days. In this atmosphere, economic assistance from the world community can show that peace provides a direct economic benefit and that the world stands behind the peace. Large-scale U.S. support, on the order of post–Camp David aid to Israel and Egypt, can demonstrate the strength of America's commitment to the peace partners.

The U.S. aid program to the core peace process partners has many interesting aspects, but what is relevant to this study is what impact the aid program has on the diplomacy of the peace process itself. The main questions to ask about aid and the peace process are: How much difference do existing U.S. aid flows make? And how much stronger would the peace process be were the aid to Jordan and the Palestinian Authority (PA) substantially larger? As usual with counterfactual questions about political issues, no clear-cut methodology exists for deriving a precise answer. The best approach is instead to list the ways aid might have made a difference and the offsetting factors.

THE PALESTINIAN AUTHORITY

Aid to Palestinians has been one of the most controversial parts of the U.S. assistance program, both because of congressional skepticism about aiding Yasir Arafat's apparatus and because of complaints that miserly aid flows have undercut the peace process by depriving Palestinians of the prosperity they expected after the signing of the Oslo accords. The complaints raise a number of interrelated policy issues about the size and composition of the aid program, mostly in the nature of speculation about whether a different kind of aid program would make a difference in the peace process:

- Is the essential problem the size of the aid package? Would substantially more aid make a real difference in living standards, and would that reinforce the peace and undercut Oslo opponents?

- How appropriate is aid, given concerns about PA performance, including continuing problems of fraud and corruption, as well as its spotty record on the all-important security issues? Should the PA be trusted with U.S. aid funds or should the money go directly to humanitarian organizations with a better track record for helping the poor?

- Should aid targeted for economic and political reform create more effective governance that makes peace more durable (such as a transparent and systematically enforced body of law that, *inter alia*, governs interaction with Israel and Israelis)? Or would such focus on governance create resentment about U.S. interference in

Palestinian affairs and perceived double standards between the treatment of Israel and the PA?

- Would aid targeted more explicitly on peace process concerns, such as improving police performance or reaching agreement on Gaza–West Bank transit routes, make much difference in the parties' willingness to reach agreement on these politically contentious issues?

Background

Since 1975, the United States has had an aid program in the West Bank and Gaza. The program was quite small until then–Secretary of State George Shultz announced in 1983 that U.S. peace process policy would focus on the quality of life in the territories.[1] The quality of life initiative was a by-product of Shultz's disillusionment with political efforts toward peace. While welcoming the interest in their well-being, many in the Palestinian community saw the quality of life initiative as a ploy to substitute economics for peace.

U.S. Aid as a Small Component of the International Effort. International interest in aid for the West Bank and Gaza had been building during the 1980s, but it soared after the October 1991 Madrid conference. In conjunction with the Regional Economic Development Working Group (REDWG) organized at Madrid, donors began to prepare several proposals for aid to the Palestinian territories. The principal actors in this process were the Europeans. The United States encouraged Europe to take the lead on providing aid to Palestinians, and Europe responded eagerly. European countries individually and the European Community (EC, now European Union, or EU) as a whole were motivated in part by charitable purposes and a desire to support the peace process. In addition, they hoped to use their offers of aid to gain a seat at the diplomatic table.

After the signing of the Israeli–Palestinian Declaration of Principles (DOP) in 1993, U.S. interest in aid to the Palestinians increased sharply. Washington worked to sideline the existing processes, such as the European-led REDWG, in favor of events that gave a higher profile to the U.S. role. The United States played a key role in organizing aid sessions for the Palestinians—sessions typically called on short notice with little preparation and without making much use of the detailed work that had been done previously. Even so, the United States has made relatively smaller pledges of aid and has been a much less significant donor to the Palestinians than have the Europeans. In October 1993, the United States pledged a five-

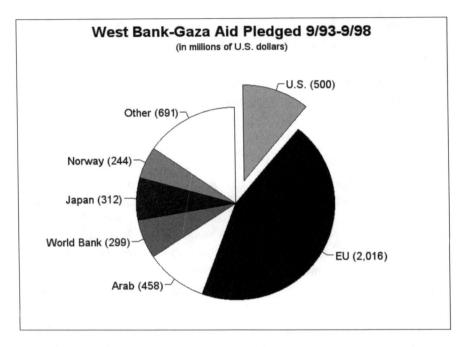

West Bank-Gaza Aid Pledged 9/93-9/98
(in millions of U.S. dollars)

U.S. (500)
Other (691)
Norway (244)
Japan (312)
World Bank (299)
Arab (458)
EU (2,016)

year, $500-million program, including $125 million in Overseas Private Investment Corporation (OPIC) credit guarantees as well as $375 million in grant funding. That pledge was 11.9 percent of the total $4.2 billion pledged during the five years from September 1993 through September 1998. According to PA data, the other large pledges were from the EU and its member countries ($2,016 million), Arab states and organizations ($458 million), Japan ($312 million), and Norway ($244 million). [2]

Turning from pledges to actual disbursements, PA data show that, in the five years from September 1993 through September 1998, the United States disbursed $345 million, or 13.8 percent of the $2,506 million disbursed then. Other large disbursers of aid were the EU and its member countries ($1,107 million), Japan ($306 million), Norway ($221 million), and Arab states and organizations ($216 million).

Although the United States was not the largest donor, its pressure on other countries likely helped to increase the amount of money pledged and disbursed from at least some of them. European countries would probably have made as large an effort for the Palestinians independent of U.S. urging, but that may not have been the case for Arab countries and the East European and smaller Asian donors. The size of the pledge from Arab states and organizations was in no small part a result of U.S. pressure, although the Arab pledge was not matched by Arab disbursements. In fact,

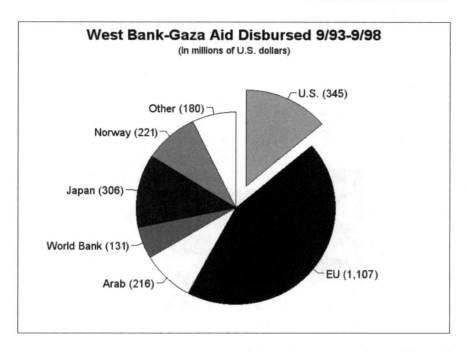

West Bank-Gaza Aid Disbursed 9/93-9/98
(in millions of U.S. dollars)

U.S. (345)
Other (180)
Norway (221)
Japan (306)
World Bank (131)
Arab (216)
EU (1,107)

during the five years after the signing of the DOP, Norway alone disbursed more aid to the West Bank and Gaza than did all Arab states and organizations combined. It is interesting to speculate whether the reasons were technical—Arab aid organizations sometimes work slowly—or political.

Huge Aid Flows. U.S. policy has been concerned about the enormity of the global aid program for Palestinians. The funds disbursed by all donors during the first five years after Oslo, according to PA data, totaled $2.5 billion. Those disbursements included $947 million for public investment; $450 million for technical assistance; $517 million for transitional and budgetary support; and $591 million for other areas including employment generation, equipment supply, in-kind aid, and private sector support.

The aid disbursed in 1997, $545 million, was $203 per person and was the equivalent of 15 percent of the Palestinian gross national product (GNP)—both levels being extraordinarily high by international standards.[3] By comparison, aid to sub-Saharan Africa in 1996 was $26 per person and 5 percent of GNP, while that for India was $2 per person and 0.6 percent of GNP.[4] In other words, aid to the PA was much greater than that to much poorer countries, both on a per capita basis and as a percent of GNP.

Moreover, the PA data understate the aid received by the West Bank

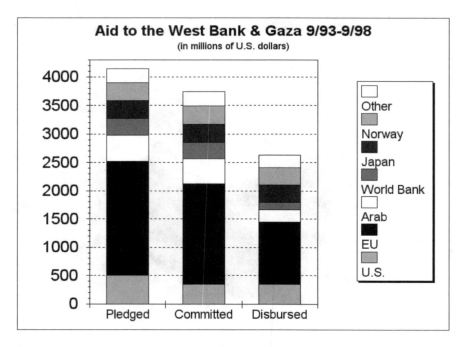

Aid to the West Bank & Gaza 9/93-9/98
(in millions of U.S. dollars)

and Gaza, because the data evidently exclude the regular nondevelopment expenditures of the UN Relief and Works Agency (UNRWA). UNRWA "runs parallel systems of education and health care for the refugee population," providing 40 percent as much health care to Palestinians as does the PA.[5] UNRWA spent $140 million for the West Bank and Gaza in 1997, above and beyond the $545 million in aid recorded by the PA in 1997.[6] Adding in UNRWA aid produces total aid of $685 million a year, or $255 per capita. The United States is the largest donor to UNRWA, providing $85 million of its $273 million 1997 regular budget.

The aid received has been well in excess of pre-Oslo estimates of aid needed. As part of the post-Madrid process, a World Bank team visited the territories in early 1993 and estimated that the public sector would need $1.44 billion committed—$1.35 billion for public investment and $90 million for technical assistance—during 1994–1998.[7] (Note that the bank based its estimate on *commitments*, which are agreements as to where and for what to spend aid money, rather than *disbursements*, which are actual checks issued.) In 1994, the bank revised its estimate—to include start-up costs and boost spending—to $1.2 billion over three years, which would have translated into $2.0 billion for five years.[8] Actual commitments during the five years, however, were $3.7 billion—183 percent of the bank's expanded 1994 estimate.

It is not clear that the Palestinian economy could have absorbed more aid than that which it has received. In 1994–1996, annual aid packages averaged $510 million, whereas public investment averaged $137 million a year according to one estimate, or $70 million a year according to another.[9] That discrepancy suggests both that the PA has not been able to put aid to use for development projects and that funding was not a constraint on economic development projects. If the aid did not go for investment, what did it help to fund? As a World Bank–financed economic study shows, the aid—along with funds Israel forwarded to the PA from taxes Palestinians paid in Israel—made public sector growth possible: from 1993 to 1996, the number of civil servants more than tripled, from 22,000 to 75,000. The study's authors deplore the economic implications of this excessive spending made possible by aid: "A strategy that places little in public investment and supports a larger-than-needed civil service in the midst of a weakened private sector, not only fails to invest in the future, but also taxes future growth."[10]

Indeed, the economic problems that could come from excessive aid were foreseen by economists in 1993 at the time of the signing of the DOP. Stanley Fischer, formerly chief economist for the World Bank and currently second in command (as first deputy managing director) at the International Monetary Fund (IMF), warned in 1993, "Massive amounts of aid (more than 12–15 percent of GNP) could overwhelm the fledgling Palestinian administration and lead to greater economic dependence."[11] In fact, aid in 1997 was 15 percent of GNP. World Bank economists therefore warned that "foreign assistance–led growth . . . can wreak havoc."[12]

Nevertheless, although the excessive aid may have been economically counterproductive, the high aid levels may have contributed to the peace process. Employing an extra 53,000 Palestinians in the civil service may have reinforced the legitimacy and authority of the PA at a time when it was taking politically difficult steps and facing opposition from those hostile to the peace process. Moreover, the employment may have offset some of the dissatisfaction about the post-Oslo recession, thereby sapping anger that could otherwise have been directed against Israel. In other words, the large aid program may have been a case of political motives trumping economic rationales.

Reasons for the Perception of a Failed Aid Program. Given that aid to the Palestinians has been quite substantial, one might ask why there is a widespread impression among Palestinians that the donors have not lived up to their responsibilities. Three reasons predominate.

The first is inflated expectations. In October 1993, the United States organized an aid-pledging session in Washington. In the call for that session, Secretary of State Warren Christopher said, "We are confident these needs [of the Palestinians] can be met. [The aid will] breathe life into the Israeli–Palestinian Declaration [by providing] quick and vividly . . . tangible improvements in the security and daily lives of the Palestinians and Israelis."[13] The session was pronounced a smashing success, with pledges to disburse $3 billion over five years; later pledges increased the total to $4 billion. U.S. policymakers paid no attention to experiences with such pledges regarding other parts of the world—an experience which shows that aid arrives much more slowly than promised at such pledging sessions.[14] Few if any statements on the public record warned that improvements would come only over time and only if Palestinians adopted sound economic policies. No evidence exists that policymakers considered the negative impact of unrealized expectations from the euphoric atmosphere after that aid-pledging session.

Yet, within less than a year of the October 1993 pledging session, disillusionment had set in among Palestinians. In November 1994, Terje Larsen, the UN undersecretary general for Palestinian territories, judged, "The donor effort is a failure; the strategy wrong, the priorities wrong, and the timetable wrong.[15] He went on, "The gap between expectations and delivery is so large, so critical, and unless donors get together to deliver, the peace process will fail."[16] This view was echoed by PA officials; Tony Zahlan, an official of the Palestinian Council for Development and Reconstruction (PECDAR), blamed the donors for the territories' economic problems, saying, "We have a situation of total disaster."[17] Hassan Abdel Rahman, the PA representative in Washington, summarized the negative impact of the large pledges followed by few results:

> The problem is that the masses of people in Gaza and the West Bank don't understand how the aid works. They hear the figure $100 million, and they think that President [Bill] Clinton has given Chairman [Yasir] Arafat a check or a satchel full of money. Then they want to know what Arafat has done with the money—why it hasn't reached them. The rumors start that he just put it in his pocket and is spending it on himself and his cronies.[18]

Second, although the PA's needs were greatest in its earliest months, the aid program got off to a slow start. Almost immediately after the October 1993 pledging session, the PA realized that it did not have the money it needed to pay its civil servants or police. The problem was highlighted at the December 1993 Consultative Group meeting, as a result of which the World Bank organized in January 1994 a special donors' conference at which participants agreed to establish a special fund—the Johan Jørgen Holst Fund for Start-Up and Recurrent Costs—to finance salaries and operating costs.[19] The Holst Fund eventually disbursed $212 million for PA recurrent spending and $37 million for employment-generating projects.[20] But the World Bank was not prepared to pay police salaries, so additional funds had to be found for that, provided by reluctant donors—no aid agency likes funding police—and coordinated through UNRWA. The end result was that, in the crucial early months, the Palestinian public and the new PA officials were constantly hearing about shortfalls in donor funding and the inability of the PA to meet its bills.

Aside from the immediate crisis over salaries, the aid program was plagued by a gap between promises of quick disbursement of development funds and the reality of slow starts to the projects. Despite their pledges, national and international agencies did not in fact waive their usual procedures.[21] Indeed, given that the aid community had mounds of studies from the 1991–1993 REDWG process laying out in detail numerous project proposals, the pace of disbursement was slow even by the standards of aid organizations. An impressive amount of ill-will was created with the PA and with Palestinian public opinion by the delays in aid flows, even though those delays are normal for the largely inefficient aid agencies. Furthermore, PA institutions were established slowly, which is precisely what the experiences of other weak governments would suggest (reconstructing governments after civil war or societal collapse has provided much experience on this point since the end of the Cold War).

Third, the Palestinian economy has done poorly despite the aid. Income declined after the DOP, and one must ask whether aid prevented a faster decline. Intriguingly, the economy did relatively well in 1994, the year in which complaints about the ineffectiveness of aid took root: output rose 10.8 percent, faster than the 4.3 percent population growth, while income, including the income from workers in Israel, rose 3.9 percent.[22] Over the five-year period 1994–1998, however, annual output rose on average 0.8 percent—well below the population growth rate. Income (real GNP) did even worse, falling 0.9 percent on average in 1994–1998, primarily because of the decline in income from work in Israel. Combining the declining income and the rising population, per capita income fell 23.5 percent from 1994 through 1998.

In fact, the economy would have fallen further and faster without aid, but it is hard for ordinary Palestinians to take much comfort in that argument. For one thing, the positive impact of the aid was so small as to be negligible compared to the negative impact of Israeli closures and inappropriate PA policies. Indeed, some Palestinians interviewed complained that the aid programs are, in their words, financing Israeli closures—that is, they sufficiently alleviate the humanitarian suffering (and associated potential for a political explosion) that Israel is able to avoid an international outcry against the closures. That may be exaggerated, but it is certainly true that the scale of the aid program offsets some of the problems caused by the closures and that Israel has therefore had to worry less about adverse reactions to the closures than it would have were there no aid.

Who Administers Aid: NGOs, USAID, or the PA? Before the DOP, U.S. aid to the Palestinians was provided primarily through nongovernmental organizations (NGOs) and UNRWA.[23] In Fiscal Year (FY) 1993 (ending September 30, 1993), the U.S. government provided NGOs with $27 million and provided an additional $68 million for UNRWA.[24] At that time, the United States was the major funder for these activities; one estimate is that in 1992, NGOs spent a total (from all sources) of $80 million in the territories, while another source says it was between $170 million and $240 million.[25] Much of the money financed social services, especially schools and hospitals; much less went to fund physical infrastructure projects or support for agriculture, industry, or trade. Many of the NGOs were effective aid providers, in that they ran cost-efficient service agencies that reached poor people. Yet, some were also used, perhaps inadvertently, by the anti–peace process opposition, especially by Islamists who used the NGOs' hospitals and schools to generate goodwill and to win recruits.[26]

After the DOP, the nascent PA was determined to take over many of the functions previously performed by NGOs in the Palestinian territories. The PA was generally suspicious of the NGOs, seeing many as Hamas-controlled, and it therefore insisted on tight control over the NGOs and mandated that aid be channeled via the government.[27] The result, not surprisingly, has been shrinking funds for Palestinian NGOs. PA data show aid to NGOs during the five years from September 1993 through September 1998 averaging $49 million a year.[28] NGOs have therefore had to curtail the services they provide; for example, NGOs ran 210 health clinics in the rural West Bank in 1992 but only 128 in 1996.[29] In short, the provision of social services in the PA areas has shifted from NGOs to the PA.

Although overall international aid has shifted away from NGOs to the PA, U.S. aid has followed a different pattern. Like other donors, the United

States has reduced its funding for NGOs. Yet, rather than working through the PA, the U.S. Agency for International Development (USAID) has directly implemented the formerly NGO-run projects itself, which is a rather unique position for the organization—and a daunting administrative challenge. Congress has been unenthusiastic about providing direct aid to the PA (or making U.S. contributions to international organizations that aid the PA), which is permitted only if the president waives several restrictive laws by certifying that the Palestine Liberation Organization is abiding by its commitments to Israel, as provided for in the PLO Commitments Compliance Act of 1989 and the Middle East Peace Facilitation Act (MEPFA) of 1993, 1994, and 1995.[30] The MEPFAs applied only for a specified period and have lapsed, but Congress remains strongly opposed to giving direct aid to the PA.

The United States has, however, provided some funds that are, in effect, direct contributions to the PA budget. Shortly after the signing of the DOP, the United States made a $25 million contribution to the World Bank–administered Holst Fund to pay for the transition costs of establishing the PA, and it also provided the PA police with 200 vehicles, blankets, and boots with a total value of $4 million.[31] Other than those funds, the U.S. aid program's main expenditures since the DOP have been on the Gaza water supply, housing, private enterprise support, humanitarian relief (such as the contributions to UNRWA), and democracy promotion.

The 1998 Decision to Increase Aid. In September 1998, as preparations began for the Wye Plantation summit, U.S. interest in economic assistance to the PA increased. After Clinton and Arafat met on September 29, White House press secretary Michael McCurry announced,

> The president and the chairman focused on what is arguably a very important part of the future for the Palestinian people under the peace agreements that have been reached. And that is the level of economic assistance that will be there for the people of West Bank and the Gaza.[32]

In November 1998, the United States organized a session in Washington to pledge additional assistance to the PA. The session was designed to provide a quick reinforcement for the Wye River Memorandum and to maximize credit given to the United States for increased aid to the PA, by taking advantage of donors' plans to pledge higher levels of aid at a long-planned Consultative Group scheduled for February 1999. The United States announced that it would, over the five years 1999–2003, increase its aid by a total of $400 million over the usual flow of $100 million a year, with the full increase apparently being funded in 1999.[33] Other donors also announced pledges totaling $3 billion, but it is difficult to evaluate what that means. At the maximum, it could mean a $3 billion increase pledged for the next five years compared to the $4 billion pledged for the last five years. Given the usual delays in committing and disbursing aid as well as the problem of finding additional uses for aid in light of the already high levels of aid the PA receives, it will be ambitious to increase aid disbursements to $900 million a year compared to the current $500 million a year. At $900 million, allowing for population growth that brings the Palestinian population to 3.0 million in 2000, aid would be the equivalent of $300 per person per year.

Policy Issues

The main lesson to be learned from the PA aid history is the degree to which political problems can be created by unrealistic expectations. Unfortunately, experience suggests that this is a lesson that U.S. policymakers will not easily absorb. During George Bush's presidency, Washington policymakers fed unrealistic expectations about aid to the former Eastern bloc; the subsequent disappointment has been a political problem in several countries, feeding nationalist backlashes against Western-style institutions and against close ties with the West. The first Clinton administration led to equally unrealistic expectations among Palestinians, with equally unfortunate results. It is important not to repeat this mistake in the course of the latest exercise in increasing aid to the Palestinians.

The aid program has not been able to reverse the decline in the Palestinian economy since Oslo. Even if aid (from all the donors combined) is increased to the extraordinary level of $300 per person per year—50 percent more than the $200 per person per year in economic aid Israel receives—it is unrealistic to anticipate that aid will spark a Palestinian economic revival. The prospects for the Palestinian economy depend primarily on the state of economic relations with Israel and on the soundness of PA policies. Nevertheless, aid inflows can mitigate what would otherwise be a sharper popular Palestinian dissatisfaction with the peace process, and in this way aid helps the peace process.

Too much attention has been given to the size of the aid program, both in terms of the overall aid package for the territories and in terms of the U.S. part of that package. In fact, as already mentioned, aid to the Palestinians is extraordinarily high, both by comparison to the aid given to others and in relation to what the Palestinian economy can absorb. A grave danger exists that further increases will create an unhealthy dependency on aid, encouraging a bloated government bureaucracy and discouraging attention to creating a healthy business environment. The record to date is not encouraging: The PA has not used funds effectively and has done little to encourage the kinds of private development that could replace dependence on aid. Better PA economic policies would result in greater economic impact from aid, but that is not the highest U.S. priority in relation to the PA.

More important than the size of the aid package is deciding what are the key objectives of the aid program. To date, U.S. aid has been channeled through NGOs or has been directly administered by USAID and has been destined for economic development, humanitarian relief, and democracy promotion. The question is whether this is the most effective way to promote the peace process. The implicit assumption underlying the current U.S. aid program is that helping the PA as an institution is unimportant and that the most important problems that can be breached with aid are poverty, suffering, and authoritarianism. It is not clear that this implicit assumption is correct. It could be argued that the more important peace process obstacles are the strength of the radical opposition, the PA's inability or unwillingness to implement the peace accords, and insufficient PA counterterrorism efforts. Aid could be an efficient instrument for overcoming some of these obstacles, but it is possible that there may be inconsistencies between overcoming these obstacles on the one hand and alleviating poverty, suffering, and authoritarianism on the other hand. The issue for U.S. policy is which is more important.

One key barrier to peace has been the strength of the radical opposition as compared to that of Arafat and his mainstream political organization, Fatah. It is not apparent whether U.S. aid to promote democracy, and thereby provide fuller opportunities for the opposition to make itself heard, alleviates or worsens this problem. Certainly the PA is an imperfect democracy, but it is by no means clear that those imperfections are the key barrier to peace—and it is worth bearing in mind that Arafat is a popular leader who might well receive majority support for strong presidential rule, even in a perfect democracy. Under present circumstances, therefore, the United States should not concentrate its aid program on promoting democracy. If, at some future point, the lack of PA democracy were to become the key barrier to peace, then it would make sense to consider making U.S. aid contingent on measured progress toward defined steps in democracy promotion. Under such circumstances, it might make sense to provide a tranche of cash aid when, for example, the PA holds municipal elections, and another tranche after it enacts a basic law protecting freedom of expression. At this stage, however, providing more directed incentives for PA compliance with its Oslo-related obligations, especially those related to security, is arguably much more important for the peace process than is promoting full democracy in the PA.

A second major problem for the peace process has been the PA's lack of ability or of will to implement its obligations under the various peace accords. The PA argues that its institutional weakness has impeded its ability to take strong measures against violent peace process opponents. A different interpretation is that the PA leadership has been unwilling to make unpopular concessions to Israel that might attract the opposition of vocal pressure groups. Whatever the mix of inability and unwillingness, giving aid directly to the PA—as distinct from financing NGOs—could help. Such aid would allow the PA to carry out development projects much in the same way as ordinary governments use U.S. aid funds, and it would make the PA subject to all the same strict procedures to prevent fraud and to ensure that all funds are used for the purposes agreed to between PA and USAID. Allowing the PA to carry out projects on its own would help it to build institutional capabilities. It would also give the PA more political clout—through jobs and services provided—which could make the PA more willing to take politically difficult steps.

A third barrier to peace has been insufficient efforts to combat terrorism. Immediately after the 1993 DOP, Congress required that aid to the PA be contingent on determinations that the PA was fighting terrorism. That did not prove to be an effective means of encouraging more PA counterterrorism efforts; instead, it invited reports from the administration that certified compliance. A more effective approach would provide direct inducements—positive or negative—to the PA leadership to take specific steps to counter terrorism, which would make more concrete the commitments the PA has made in this regard. This will be hard to do and may be impossible, but it is worth exploring.

One method for providing cash aid that is worth considering would be to spell out the specific steps desired and establish quantifiable targets, making the release of funds contingent on performance. The release of U.S. aid tied to quantified progress on political objectives has been used in other parts of the world, for example in the Andean countries, where U.S. cash aid is tied to the fulfillment of drug-eradication goals (so many dollars in aid for so many hectares of coca plants eradicated). Determining which steps are the most important and setting quantitative goals for each such step is a difficult process, but it has the merit of providing a yardstick by which to measure PA counterterrorism efforts. Targets could include an increase in the arrests of those sought for crimes, confiscation of weapons, transfer or incarceration of terrorists, faster disposition of cases, the passing of clear counterterrorism laws, and the training of counterterrorism police. This approach might give Arafat a more direct and immediate reason to carry out the desired actions, as well as a clearer explanation to Palestinians as to why he was carrying out actions that may not be popular.

In addition to providing the PA an incentive to fulfill specific peace-promoting objectives, cash aid would provide Arafat with the resources to create political support for his program. This would signal greater U.S. political support for the elected PA government. In addition, it would free the PA from cumbersome and bureaucratic U.S. procurement procedures and the detailed U.S. government accounting standards—although some would argue that these procedures and standards, even if externally imposed on a democratic government that resists them, are important for transparency and accountability. Cash aid, on the other hand, would make it impossible to insist on such standards, for cash is fungible. Even if the United States insisted on strict accounting of what use was made of its cash aid, that aid would free up funds Arafat could use for other purposes. Therefore, providing cash aid could be the same as financing PA corruption. Ideally, the PA will implement the desired economic (accounting and anticorruption) reforms, so cash aid could be provided to reinforce the PA politically. If the ideal does not happen, however, one must set priorities. In such an imperfect world, the essential question that should govern whether to allocate cash aid to the PA is which would best serve the peace process, improving PA accounting standards and reducing corruption, or providing an incentive to fulfill peace-promoting objectives and helping to expand Arafat's political base so that he can afford to risk concessions to Israel.

Another disadvantage of any direct financial support to the PA is that U.S. payments to Arafat might make him appear excessively dependent on the United States, and the United States would be viewed as being behind every step Arafat took. This risk was well illustrated in the interviews the authors had with some Palestinians, who complained that U.S. assistance to and cooperation with the Palestinian Security Services (PSS) was converting those organizations into field offices of the Federal Bureau of Investigation and Central Intelligence Agency and that PSS torture of prisoners (as alleged by the interviewees) must have been with techniques learned from their U.S. counterparts.

A third potential disadvantage can be seen in the existing USAID program to promote democratization in the Palestinian areas, which has assisted with the drafting of a basic law (a form of constitution). Not surprisingly, the draft basic law approved by the Palestinian Legislative Council declares Jerusalem the capital of Palestine. If the United States tied aid disbursal to adoption of the basic law, Washington would either have to approve disbursal of money for a law containing such a provision—angering Israelis—or it would have to insist on vetting the basic law for content—angering Palestinians.

To conclude on a more positive note, the U.S. aid program has demonstrated that the United States cares about the well-being of the Palestinians. That has lessened the popular Palestinian impression that the United States is concerned only about Israel. The U.S. aid program contributes to the image of the United States as an honest broker between Israel and the Palestinians, and for that reason, it helps Washington to mediate and promote its role in the peace process. This is a welcome change from the Palestinian attitudes toward the United States as expressed in the 1970s and 1980s. At that time, U.S. concentration on economic issues was seen by some nationalist Palestinians as a ploy to divert attention from political concerns. The reaction to Secretary Shultz's 1983–1984 quality of life initiative, mentioned earlier, demonstrates that Palestinians may be suspicious of economic initiatives during periods of no progress on the political side of the peace process, and that Palestinians as a whole place much more importance on politics than on economics.

Another plus for the U.S. government is its success at receiving credit for mobilizing funds for the Palestinians—a credit well-deserved with regard to Arab donors but not especially appropriate with respect to the Europeans, who have been the main donors to the Palestinians. That Europe pays the bills while Washington calls the shots in the peace process could be seen as a financial success for the United States, but it has engendered ill-will among Europeans, which in turn has reduced their willingness to work together with the United States on aid issues.

JORDAN

After the 1994 Jordanian–Israeli peace treaty, Jordan did receive U.S. aid—albeit on a smaller scale than that provided to Egypt, much less to Israel, after the Camp David accords. Jordan is of course a smaller country than Egypt or Israel, so the aid should be calculated on a per capita basis or as a percentage of GNP. By both those measures, however, the U.S. aid provided to Jordan was about half that given to Egypt after Camp David. The initial composition of the aid was primarily debt relief and excess military equipment; in 1997, Washington added a five-year program for substantial cash aid. Both because the aid package was smaller than the Jordanian public had hoped and because the initial aid had little immediate economic impact, the Jordan aid program has not had as much of a positive political effect as did the Egypt aid program. The Jordan aid program is, however, slated for a substantial increase in 1999.

Background

The United States has not historically been a large donor to Jordan, which has relied more on other industrial countries and oil-rich Arab states. In the 1980s, U.S. aid to Jordan averaged $110 million a year, of which $60 million was military.[34] In the early 1990s, U.S.–Jordanian relations suffered because of Jordan's neutral- to pro-Iraqi stance during Operations Desert Shield and Desert Storm. During 1991–1993, U.S. aid to Jordan averaged only $60 million a year, of which $17 million was military.

In October 1993, however, President Clinton publicly pledged to provide relief of Jordan's debt to the United States.[35] Initially, that took the form of rescheduling $400 million in the context of a Paris Club accord, an agreement among the major industrial nations to provide debt relief for any country with an IMF-supported economic reform program. In his address to the Jordanian parliament after the signing of the Israel–Jordan Peace Treaty, President Clinton promised, "We have pledged to forgive all of Jordan's debt to our own government, and we have encouraged—indeed, urged—other countries to do the same."[36] The United States thus forgave $698 million in debt in several tranches from 1994 through 1997.[37] The write-off reduced Jordan's debt service obligations by approximately $30 million a year from what they would have been, had debt reschedulings been used instead. In addition, President Clinton declared Jordan a major non-NATO ally, and Jordan was granted excess military equipment from the stocks the United States was discarding because of the end of the Cold War. In July 1996, sixteen F-16 Block 15 air defense fighters—planes that had been in storage since June 1994 after serving the Air National Guard—were transferred to the Jordanian military.[38]

By 1997, a consensus emerged in the U.S. government that more had to be done to help Jordan, but budgetary constraints threatened the administration's proposal to boost aid from $40 million in FY1997 to $70 million in FY1998.[39] The United States therefore asked Israeli policymakers whether Israel would be willing to forego some aid it received under what had in practice become a fixed annual allocation, so Washington could increase aid to Jordan. The result was the establishment of a $100 million Middle East Peace and Stability Fund in June 1997, to provide additional resources for countries making a positive contribution to the peace process (read: Jordan), using U.S. aid funds that would otherwise have gone to Israel and Egypt, and both country's aid levels were cut $50 million from the previous year. More technically, Israel returned $50 million it had already received while Egypt's "pipeline" of undisbursed funds from the previous year's allocations was cut $65.67 million, both to finance the Middle East Peace and Stability Fund and to ensure that overall aid to the region fit under a cap imposed by Section 586 of U.S. Public Law 105-118.[40]

As part of the 1997 program, President Clinton made a five-year commitment for expanded U.S. aid to Jordan. For its part, Congress not only approved the proposed reallocation but added funds to the administration's request for $100 million in aid to Jordan. Thanks to those funds, the U.S. aid program for Jordan rose to $158 million in FY1997 (including $32 million in military aid), $192 million in FY1998 (including $52 million in military aid), and an appropriated $198 million for FY1999 (including $47 million in military aid).[41] Jordan was also provided "draw-down authority" to receive excess military items worth up to $25 million a year, meaning that the 1999 total aid plus draw-down was to be $223 million, before the November 1998 increase discussed below.

It is instructive to compare the Jordan aid program after the 1994 peace treaty to the aid programs for Egypt and Israel after the 1978 Camp David summit and subsequent treaty. Extra military aid was given to both Egypt and Israel in 1979—$1.5 billion to Egypt and $3 billion to Israel, to facilitate the transition of the Egyptian military from Soviet to Western equipment and to offset costs imposed on Israel by the return of Sinai airfields. With that supplement to the regular aid flows, total U.S. aid to Egypt that year was 15 percent of the Egyptian GNP; for Israel, the comparable figure was 27 percent. Over the next five years (1980–1984), the two received aid each year that averaged 7.5 percent of Egypt's GNP and 9.4 percent of Israel's. Put another way, that aid averaged $71 for each Egyptian and $960 for each Israeli (at 1998 prices). By contrast, the aid program for Jordan started slower and stayed lower. The Jordan aid program did not increase until two years after the peace treaty, not immediately. The 1997–1999 aid to Jordan, averaging $183 million a year, was 3 percent of GNP, less than half the level of aid that Egypt received after the Camp David treaty. And the aid to Jordan was $37 per person per year—about half the per capita aid Egypt received and 4 percent of the aid Israel received (at 1998 prices). To be sure, Jordan received debt relief and excess military equipment, but the amount it received in 1994–1996 was less than half the per capita average annual amounts Egypt has received for the same purposes over the last twenty years. In short, it seems fair to say that, after adjusting for the relative sizes of the two countries, Jordan received aid after its peace treaty with Israel that was about half the amount Egypt received after Camp David.

Of course, the lower level of aid given to Jordan compared to that given to Egypt could be evaluated against the background of each country's economic needs. Here there is a paradox: Jordan seemed less needy (it had in 1994 less absolute poverty and a higher per capita income than Egypt had in 1979), but Jordanians were more upset about their country's economic circumstances. The Jordanian national psyche is still scarred by the sharp economic crisis in the late 1980s, when per capita income fell 60 percent, largely because the end of the oil boom meant less aid for Jordan and less work in the Gulf for Jordanians. Per capita income in Jordan has grown since that crisis, but it is still only half its 1987 peak, and Jordanians still compare their current reduced economic circumstances to those boom days. As a result, when Jordanians thought about the prosperity that peace with Israel might bring, they may have had in mind a quick return to the roaring 1980s when per capita incomes were twice their current level. Faced with that sort of expectation, the small aid programs and the even smaller inflows of investment funds inevitably were disappointing.

If one argument for aid to Jordan is to reverse the income decline of the last decade, another is that peace imposed costs on its economy, somewhat similar to the costs Israel sustained after Camp David when it had to give up large airfields in the Sinai. What Jordan had to give up was not airfields, but seignorage—the advantages a government draws from printing money.[42] The money held by the public is essentially an interest-free loan to the government. Prior to the DOP, Palestinians in the West Bank and Gaza held between $400 million and $800 million in Jordanian dinars, which was like a multimillion-dollar interest-free loan to the Jordanian Central Bank.[43] The large holdings of dinars were necessary because of the extremely poor banking services in the territories, owing to Israeli restrictions and Palestinians' refusal to use branches of Israeli banks. After the DOP, the Palestinians were freer to establish commercial banks, which within five years attracted $2 billion in deposits. The result was that holdings of dinar notes fell sharply. Not only did Jordan lose the interest-free "loan," but it had to pay out in foreign exchange when the dinars were converted into dollars for deposit in the new banks. In other words, Jordan sustained a substantial transitional cost from the establishment of the Palestinian Authority.

In late 1998, the Clinton administration decided to increase aid to Jordan by a further $300 million over three years.[44] The proposal was for $100 million in cash economic aid and $200 million in military aid, primarily equipment suitable for guarding Jordan's borders, including materiel needed to stop smugglers on the Jordan–Iraq border. To the previously scheduled aid level of $223 million a year, the provisional plan is to increase aid over three years by a total of about $375 million ($200 million in economic aid and $175 million in military aid, including draw-down). That would bring the annual aid package to $75 a person, just over the $71 per capita level Egypt received in the five years after Camp David. To match the level of aid given to Egypt as a share of GNP would require $550 million a year (7.5 percent of GNP).

Policy Issues

The United States aid program to Jordan has not been the kind of political success that the aid program to Egypt was after Camp David. The reasons are many: The program started slowly, it was smaller than in Egypt, and it had to overcome a negative economic atmosphere when the high initial expectations for a post-peace economic boom were not realized.

As of late 1998, the provisional plan is to provide Jordan with economic and military aid at the same level that Egypt got after Camp David—$71 per capita for the three years 1999–2001, using a supplemental 1999 appropriation. Such an increase could be sustained by reprogramming resources made available by the planned reduction in aid to Israel and Egypt (aid to Israel and Egypt is likely to drop each year by $90 million from the level the year before).

The initial debt relief was an important aspect of peace with Israel in the minds of Jordanian leaders, who were acutely aware of the burden that the debt placed on the country's medium-term prospects. It is not clear if that attitude was widely shared among the population as a whole, which may have been less concerned about the burden of debt payments. Some may have expected Jordan to be able to avoid paying the debt in full, and they might have cynically seen the debt relief as putting a fine gloss on the inevitable. After all, Jordan had been able to postpone debt payments for some years through rescheduling agreements, and the experience of other highly indebted countries around the world in the 1980s and 1990s has been that such reschedulings are often a signal that the debt will never be paid in full.

Popular expectations about aid to Jordan after the peace treaty may have been inflated, though it does not appear that either the U.S. or Jordanian governments did much to encourage exaggerated expectations about aid. Quite to the contrary, there appear to have been few if any statements in 1994–1995 by high government officials that would lead one to expect large aid flows. President Clinton's speech to the Jordanian parliament after the signing of the peace treaty emphasized the economic advantages of peace; these were not presented as aid flows but as the dividends of cooperation and peace. Nevertheless, the popular expectation of peace-time prosperity seems to have included the assumption that the United States would take whatever actions were necessary to ensure that such prosperity emerged, even if that required a large U.S. aid program. In any case, when the post-treaty economic boom failed to materialize to the extent expected, blame fell in part on the United States for not providing a larger aid package.

When the United States began a larger aid program in 1997, the increase came mostly in form of cash, not more project aid. That decision was economically appropriate. Over the last decade, the Jordanian government has had a good track record for making use of aid resources for development needs, rather than subsidizing consumption or financing low-return prestige projects. That track record instills confidence in the donors that Jordan will use its cash aid as well as it uses its project aid, especially given that USAID's record for designing and implementing projects is decidedly mixed (its cumbersome procedures slow the pace and raise the costs for projects). But, for U.S. interests, even more important than the economic impact of the cash aid has been the political impact. Cash aid provides resources directly to politicians, who are—not surprisingly—appreciative of the resources put at their disposal.

Although the three-year lag between the peace treaty and the increase in U.S. cash aid had its negative side, the positive aspect was that when the aid came, it was unexpected. Senior Jordanian officials interviewed in early 1998 were unanimous in commenting that they had not anticipated the presidential request for such an aid increase nor that Congress would increase the amount appropriated beyond that which the president requested. They saw these actions not only as economically helpful but more significantly as a signal of U.S. commitment to a strategic relationship—that is, as a recognition of Jordan's strategic importance on a variety of fronts, including vis-à-vis Iraq as well as on peace process issues. Of course, regardless of the economic assistance, the Jordanian government has generally favored peace and been a strong U.S. ally. The political problem is dissatisfaction among citizens about the peace process and lack of economic gain. Immediate aid may have mitigated this.

Precisely because of Jordan's strategic position in a troubled region, the United States has an interest in a stronger Jordanian military. This interest would argue for military aid to Jordan irrespective of the peace process. Military aid to Jordan has been useful for U.S. policy toward Iraq. A stronger Jordanian army is better able to police the borders with Iraq—to prevent smuggling that undercuts the UN sanctions. U.S. aid upgraded an airfield near Iraq from which a U.S. Air Force air expeditionary force was able to operate in 1995–1996; the provision of F-16s to Jordan at that time also facilitated combined operations between the two countries' air forces. Given the high reputation of the Jordanian military's training and readiness, upgrading Jordanian weaponry and logistical infrastructure may be one of the most effective ways to improve the readiness of friendly Arab militaries to operate alongside the United States during a regional crisis— Jordanian forces might bring to such a crisis real military muscle, not just the political credibility that comes from having Arab partners. Moreover, U.S. military aid may also have reinforced the Jordanian military's willingness to work with Israel. Unlike the cold peace with Egypt, Israel's peace with Jordan involves extensive military-to-military contacts.

The actions of 1997 established a precedent that, as aid to Israel and Egypt diminishes, aid to Jordan may increase. It would not be surprising if Jordanians came to expect such a connection. That can be useful for U.S. interests in several ways, including driving home to Middle Easterners that U.S. resources for the region are limited. At the same time, it can be expected that Israel will try to reap advantages with Jordan for the redirection of the aid, presenting the U.S. aid almost as if it were an Israeli gift to Jordan. That is not in the U.S. interest, both because the United States wants to maximize the credit it receives for the aid to Jordan and because the United States does not want anyone (including Israelis) to think that Israel sets U.S. policy.

LEBANON AND SYRIA

The dilemma for U.S. aid to Lebanon is that the country is effectively controlled by the terrorism-sponsoring government of its neighbor, Syria. Particularly a problem for Washington is the strong U.S. presence in the rebuilding of the Lebanese military. The military aid program makes the Lebanese army more technically proficient for controlling southern Lebanon, which is a small part of what is needed before Israel can withdraw from its security zone in the extreme South, but it also transfers U.S. military equipment and techniques to a government that—at Syria's orders— does little to stop terrorist attacks on Israeli civilians.

The United States has not had an aid program in Syria for decades. It may seem premature to discuss what kind of aid program America might offer, given the frozen state of Israeli–Syrian negotiations. But perhaps this is precisely the right moment to draw lessons from the experiences of using aid elsewhere in the Middle East to advance the peace process, so if there is progress on the Syrian front, the best practices from elsewhere can be applied.

Lebanon

The United States has had a small aid program operating in Lebanon since the 1950s. During the civil war, projects were implemented through NGOs without direct involvement of U.S. personnel. After the Taif Accords ended the war in 1989, international interest in helping Lebanon increased, with the resumption of World Bank lending and a December 1991 World Bank–organized meeting of potential donors.[45] Yet, U.S. assistance remained low, consisting during the early 1990s mostly of food aid, support for the American University of Beirut and its hospital, and about $2 million a year in general aid. The Lebanese government devoted much effort to ambitious plans to secure massive external financing, in the hopes that it could fund the ten-year (1992–2001), $11.7 billion Horizon 2000 project for rebuilding Beirut, which was prepared with significant input from the U.S. firm Bechtel. Yet, the funding secured fell far short of Lebanese requests; in his first three years after assuming office in March 1992, businessman-turned-prime minister Rafik Hariri was able to secure only $1.9 billion in aid from all countries and international organizations. U.S. aid was limited not only for economic reasons—the plan seemed overly large—but also because of the basic political problem that Lebanon is effectively controlled by the Syrian government, which is hostile to the United States.

In early 1996, USAID was in the process of phasing out all assistance, with the last operations scheduled for 1999. Then came the devastation caused by Operation Grapes of Wrath and the Israeli attacks in April 1996. As part of the settlement of that dispute, the United States agreed to host the Friends of Lebanon conference in December 1996. At that conference, Hariri claimed that pledges for the Horizon 2000 program were raised to $3.2 billion, though the lack of details at the time cast doubt on his statement. Shortly thereafter, the United States committed itself to a five-year, $60-million development aid program for Lebanon, in addition to humanitarian aid. For FY1999, the $12-million allocation consists of $7 million for NGO-implemented reconstruction activities in rural villages, $3 million for computerization of government operations (described by USAID as democracy support), and $2 million for American University of Beirut environmental laboratories and associated facilities.[46] None of this seems particularly closely related to the peace process.

Besides its economic assistance, the United States also provides Lebanon with International Military Education and Training (IMET) aid, budgeted at $550,000 each year in FY1997–FY1999.[47] More significant has been the post-Taif reconstruction—with U.S. equipment and weapons—of the Lebanese Army. The combination of U.S. equipment, U.S. training, and joint exercises with U.S. forces has made the United States a major sponsor of the Lebanese Army.[48] The Lebanese Army has therefore become a technically more competent force. It is much less politicized than during the 1980s; for instance, units are not organized on ethnic lines. The army has been used in some politically charged operations, especially the Syrian-supported 1997 pursuit of a Hizballah splinter faction in the Bekaa Valley. There is some reason for optimism that the army could be used to restore the authority of the Lebanese government in southern Lebanon were Syria to give its support to such a venture.

Yet, the technical capability of the Lebanese Army is of little importance, as long as Syria continues to control Lebanon and to encourage armed attacks by Lebanese groups—mostly Hizballah—against Israelis. No matter how proficient the Lebanese Army may be, it will not be permitted by its Syrian masters to move against terrorists and armed extremists whose attacks serve Syrian interests. Indeed, Syria could order the Lebanese Army to shield from Israeli retaliation or preemption those extremists who attack Israelis—an example of how a stronger Lebanese Army may become a problem for U.S. interests.

For the time being, the Lebanese Army will remain subservient to the wishes of Syria, which is by no stretch of the imagination a friend of the United States. Therefore, not only is there the danger that U.S. aid will reinforce an instrument of Syrian control, but there is also the risk that Syria's military may learn, via the training provided the Lebanese Army, about U.S. equipment and U.S. techniques. Bearing all that in mind, however, continued limited U.S. support to the Lebanese Army seems appropriate as one element in creating the preconditions for an eventual Lebanese–Israeli peace.

Syria

Two major barriers have prevented U.S. aid to Syria, or acquiescence in aid by international organizations: Syria's support for terrorists and extremists who attack Israelis, and its economic policies.

Syria's tacit support is essential to the functioning of Hizballah in Lebanon, which launches armed attacks on Israelis, including Israeli civilians. The U.S. government may not always judge these actions to be terroristic, but they are certainly harmful to the peace process. In addition, Syria has been designated a state sponsor of terrorism since the U.S. Department of State started preparing a list of such states in 1979. Recent State Department *Patterns of Global Terrorism* reports have stated, in the words of the 1998 report, "There is no evidence that Syrian officials have been directly involved in planning or executing international terrorist attacks since 1986," but Syria still harbors terrorists and provides facilities for their use.[49] Syria's presence on the terrorism list prevents it from receiving U.S. aid or U.S. support for aid from international organizations. Yet, the precedent of giving aid to the PA—which many in Congress considered to be a terrorist-harboring organization up to the moment the United States pledged massive aid in 1993—suggests that, were there an imminent Syrian–Israeli peace deal, the United States might decide to provide aid and play a role in mobilizing aid from others.

The other barrier to Washington providing aid is that Damascus follows a Nasserist economic policy: it has a command economy rather than a market economy, is inward-oriented rather than integrated into world markets, and remains essentially closed to foreign investors. In the words of David Butter in the *Middle East Economic Digest*, "There has been no shortage of suggestions about the kinds of reforms needed to help Syria better realize its economic potential," including a 1996 letter from leading Syrian exporter Riyad Seif.[50] But little action has ever resulted.

It is worth noting that Syria *has* been a major recipient of aid—mostly from Arab countries but also from industrial countries and international institutions—in addition to the massive military aid it received from the former Soviet Union. The Syrian government provides the IMF with reports about the grants it has received, which show large inflows during the oil boom of 1973–1985. Syria also received considerable cash grants after it agreed to participate in the allied coalition against Iraq in 1990–1991, but Syrian government data do not reflect this. In addition, Syria received a commitment for loans of $2 billion after the Gulf War, mostly from Kuwait, Saudi Arabia, the United Arab Emirates, and Japan.[51]

Despite receiving a fair amount of aid, Syria has not used the funds effectively, either during the oil boom or after the Gulf War. This may not matter much in considering whether aid could help the peace process, but it is important to the aid-giving bureaucracies, which not only help to make decisions about aid and but also would administer any aid granted. In the early 1980s, despite the massive grant inflows, Syria managed to run up an unsustainable foreign debt, on which it stopped making payments. Its arrears to Western governments and the World Bank prevented it from getting new credits from those sources for more than a decade; only in 1997 did it sign an agreement to pay off the $526 million in World Bank arrears over five years.[52] The EU included in its 1987–1991 and 1992–1996 aid programs an allocation of $350 million for Syria, but the program remained suspended because of the arrears, compounded by complaints from the European parliament about human rights abuses.[53]

The historical record offers little reason to believe that Syrian president Hafiz al-Asad would be swayed by aid.[54] He has clung stubbornly to policies harmful to Syrian development, even when that has meant forgoing substantial sums of aid; evidently he places more importance on maintaining tight political control than on ensuring economic development. It would take considerable optimism to hope that the offer of generous international aid might facilitate Syrian concessions on even the peripheral peace process issues, such as procedures to verify limits on forces near the border.

Itamar Rabinovich, the Israeli negotiator with Syria, notes with considerable delicacy that the one time the Syrians agreed to receive a U.S. envoy to discuss aid—which the Americans were promoting "as a bridge" to peace—the discussions "revealed the huge gap between the Ba'th regime's traditional approach to economic matters and the fundamental requirements of any international effort to boost the Syrian economy."[55]

At the same time, Asad will likely demand aid, on the grounds that Egypt received aid after Camp David. He is determined to get at least as good a deal as Egyptian president Anwar Sadat received. Yet, it would seem unlikely that the United States would be prepared to offer Asad that level of aid package, both because of the changed circumstances (including the lack of enthusiasm for aid in Congress) and because Asad is unlikely to follow Sadat into becoming a strategic friend of the United States. It seems more likely that the United States would encourage Europe and Gulf countries to enlarge and accelerate their aid programs for Syria.

The United States may well decide to offer Syria post-peace aid, not to facilitate concessions but to cement the peace. As happened in Jordan, peace may lead to inflated expectations among the public about prosperity being around the corner; after all, the government has found the confrontation with Israel an ever-handy excuse for explaining away privation. Unfortunately, the reality is that Syria is not going to experience an economic takeoff until government policies improve. Realizing this, U.S. officials could direct aid to the private sector rather than to large infrastructure projects, thus making aid a potential means of reinforcing civil society independent of the government.

AID COORDINATION AND MULTILATERAL INSTITUTIONS

In terms of advancing political purposes, the main role of aid coordination and of international financial institutions (IFIs)—meaning in this case the World Bank and the IMF—has been with respect to aid to the Palestinian Authority. They had a lesser role in mobilizing aid for Egypt, although they were more active in providing funds to Cairo after Camp David than they might have been without the peace accord. Peace with Israel effectively precluded Egypt from the flood of aid gushing out of the oil-rich Arab countries, so Washington pressured the IFIs to extend Egypt every consideration possible. The sums involved were quite substantial, but the political impact of the early 1980s IFI aid to Egypt pales in comparison to the political effects of the aid to the PA.

Background

The role of the World Bank in the West Bank and Gaza started with the Madrid Conference in 1991. In the immediate aftermath of the DOP, the bank encouraged unrealistic views of how quickly it and others would act, ignoring the wealth of data the bank has on implementation problems in the region. The bank implied that with greater energy by donors and the PA, aid could be disbursed faster, which was either naïve or disingenuous. The bank did nothing to identify barriers to moving faster, nor to highlight the shortcuts donors would have to accept if aid were to flow quickly—shortcuts that, in many cases, would have required them to abandon established procedures.

The donor community was quickly faced with the quandary that the PA needed financing for its recurrent budget and especially for its police force. Donors dislike funding recurrent costs and most of them absolutely refuse to become involved with security and law-enforcement issues. With active participation of the United States, the donor community therefore quickly established the Holst Fund, so donors could finance—indirectly—the PA's needs. The bank's role with the Holst Fund was key to making this work and to overcoming obstacles for donors.

Communication among donors has tended to function relatively well. The October 1993 pledging session was in large part a U.S.-orchestrated effort to get others to provide aid to consolidate the peace agreement. The lead U.S. role was not particularly resented, as the international donors were quite enthusiastic about the accord, and they recognized that only the United States could pull off a high-level session quickly. Afterwards, however, the lead in consultation among donors shifted to the World Bank. Besides its respected technical expertise, the bank was politically more acceptable to the Europeans and the Palestinians than a direct U.S. role would have been; neither wanted the United States to have a headline role. Moreover, it was difficult for the United States to argue for a more prominent role when it was not funding the PA except in special circumstances. In that respect, in fact, USAID sets a bad example. On aid coordination, rather than taking part in a concerted effort with the PA to identify overall needs and what role USAID could play in meeting them, USAID simply tells the PA what it plans to fund, even if the projects are unnecessary.

The World Bank and the IMF, in contrast, have been very involved in building up Palestinian institutions. Their role is politically more acceptable than that of the United States, in part because they can draw upon skilled Arab nationals and in part because the institutions bend over backwards to be sensitive to PA political concerns. At the same time, and to their credit, the quality of analysis from the IFIs about economic developments has been higher than that of any others looking at the Palestinian economy.

Policy Issues
The international financial institutions bear heavy responsibility for the inflated expectations after the DOP. Their staffs made unrealistic statements about the speed at which aid could be disbursed, and they provided no caveats, despite a wealth of staff research drawing on experiences around the world, about the limited impact of aid on prosperity. The strong impression is that the IFIs' behavior was based on bureaucratic interests—the desire to maximize their role in the process—rather than on dispassionate professional analyses. Also apparently important was the IFIs' desire to please their main shareholder—the United States. Thus, it may be asking too much to expect such institutions to tell the U.S. government what it does not want to hear.

On the other hand, the IFIs can bring a wealth of practical experience, including high-level technical assistance, that is politically acceptable to all sides. As a result, during difficult political times, the IFIs can function more effectively than nearly any other agencies. To the extent that political suspicions erect barriers to the implementation of aid projects, the lesson may be to enhance the role of the IFIs. That may mean leaning on the donor countries to agree to cofinance World Bank projects rather than to proceed on their own. The obvious disadvantage for the donor governments is that they want maximum publicity for their role in the projects. Moreover, the United States is in a poor position to urge cofinancing with the World Bank unless it takes the lead, rather than insisting on implementing its own projects. U.S. cofinancing for World Bank projects could be a political plus, as it could be used to feed the widespread impression that the bank is heavily influenced by the United States—an impression that helps the United States by overstating its influence.

Consultation among donors can provide the PA a platform to present its needs in a comprehensive way, but it cannot be expected to do much more than keep everyone informed on a timely basis about what others are doing with the Palestinians and what problems they are encountering. Aid coordination sessions, which by their very nature are attended primarily by aid professionals, are not the appropriate venue for discussions of political issues, like how to address security concerns that are slowing down development projects.

NOTES

1   Joyce Starr, *Development Diplomacy: U.S. Economic Assistance to the West Bank and Gaza*, Policy Paper No. 12 (Washington, D.C.: The Washington Institute for Near East Policy, 1989), pp. 2–10.

2   Ministry of Planning and International Cooperation, *1998 Third Quarterly Monitoring Report of Donors' Assistance* (hereafter: PNA, *1998 Third Quarter Donor Report*); available on the Palestinian National Authority website, http://nmopic.pa.net/reports/aid_reports/. This is the source for all data on aid to the West Bank and Gaza, unless otherwise specified.

3   The per capita figure was calculated using the Palestinian Central Bureau of Statistics (PCBS) 1997 census figure of 2.69 million inhabitants, excluding eastern Jerusalem (the population of which PCBS estimates at 0.21 million); from the PCBS website, http://www.pcbs.org/english/. Other population estimates are lower and would therefore result in higher estimates of aid per person. The GNP estimate is from Steven Barnett et al., *The Economy of the West Bank and Gaza Strip* (Washington, D.C.: International Monetary Fund, 1998), p. 6.

4   World Bank, *World Development Report 1998/99* (Washington, D.C.: World Bank, 1999), pp. 230–231.

5   Ishac Diwan and Radwan Shaban, eds., *Development Under Adversity: The Palestinian Economy in Transition* (Palestine Economic Policy Research Institute [MAS] and the World Bank, 1998), pp. 18, 31.

6   UNRWA 1999 budget data provided by UNRWA/New York.

7   World Bank, *Developing the Occupied Territories: An Investment in Peace*

(Washington, D.C.: The World Bank, 1993), vol. 1, pp. 24–25.

8   World Bank, *Emergency Assistance Program for the Occupied Territories*, 1994; Prem Garg and Samir El-Khouri, "Aiding the Development Effort for the West Bank and Gaza," *Finance and Development* (September 1994), pp. 7–9.

9   For the higher estimate, see UN Special Coordinator (UNSCO), *UNSCO Report on Economic and Social Conditions in the West Bank and Gaza Strip 1997*, p. 9, available on the UNSCO website, http://www.arts.mcgill.ca/mepp/unsco/. For the lower estimate, see Diwan and Shaban, *Development Under Adversity*, p. 7.

10 Diwan and Shaban, *Development Under Adversity*, p. 7.

11 Stanley Fischer, "Palestinians Need Home-Grown Prosperity," *Financial Times*, October 8, 1993.

12 Ishac Diwan and Michael Walton, "The Economy of the West Bank and Gaza: From Dependent to Autonomous Growth," *Finance and Development* (September 1994), p. 6.

13 Quoted in Elaine Sciolino, "U.S. To Contribute $250 Million in Aid for Palestinians," *New York Times*, September 21, 1993, p. A1.

14 See Patrick Clawson, "The Political Effect of Economic Aid to the Palestinians," *Peacewatch* no. 67, The Washington Institute for Near East Policy, September 24, 1993.

15 Julian Ozanne, "Palestinian Aid Programme 'Has Been a Failure,'" *Financial Times*, November 22, 1994, p. 4.

16 Julian Ozanne, "Aid in Time," *Financial Times*, November 25, 1994, p. 12.

17 Toby Ash, "Palestine's Crisis of Expectations," *Middle East Economic Digest (MEED)*, June 9, 1995, p. 5. See also John Goshko, "Supporters of Arafat in U.S. Say Financial Aid is Too Slow, Limited," *Washington Post*, December 27, 1994, p. A18.

18 Goshko, "Supporters of Arafat."

19 This paragraph relies heavily on Barbara Balaj, Ishac Diwan, and Bernard Philippe, "External Assistance to the Palestinians: What Went Wrong?," translated from *Politique Étrangère* 60, no. 3 (Autumn 1995).

20 World Bank, "Third Quarter 1998 Update on Bank Group Operations," available at http://www.palecon.org/.

21 Asked in November 1998 about the delays in disbursements, World Bank president James Wolfensohn said, "We have in fact at the moment got a rather good progress in terms of implementation"—highlighting that what aid bureaucracies regard as a good disbursement rate can be quite different from what politicians expected in October 1993. (Press conference by PA chairman Arafat and others at the U.S. Department of State, November 30, 1998).

22 Income and output data are from Barnett et al., *The Economy of the West Bank*

and Gaza Strip, p. 4; population and population growth are from UNSCO, *Report on Economic and Social Conditions*, p. 15.

23 Sara Roy, "U.S. Economic Aid to the West Bank and Gaza Strip: The Politics of Peace," *Middle East Policy* 4, no. 4 (Spring 1996), p. 56.

24 Clyde Mark, "Palestinians: U.S. Assistance to Palestinians," (Washington: Congressional Research Service, August 24, 1995), pp. 12, 14.

25 The lower estimate is from Avishay Braverman, et al., "The Management of Foreign Aid to the West Bank and Gaza," in Stanley Fischer and Thomas Schelling, chairs, *Securing Pace in the Middle East: Project on Economic Transition* (Cambridge, Mass.: Harvard University John F. Kennedy School of Government, Institute for Social and Economic Policy in the Middle East, 1993), p. 104, based on the United Nations Development Program (UNDP) compendium on aid, part of which is on pp. 108–112. The higher estimate is from Joachim Zaucker, Andrew Griffel, and Peter Gubser, "Toward Middle East Peace and Development: International Assistance to Palestinians and the Role of NGOs during the Transition to Civil Society," *InterAction Occasional Paper* (Washington: InterAction, December 1995), p. 17; a breakdown of that estimate, attributed to "World Bank sources," is on p. 20.

26 Denis Sullivan, "NGOs in Palestine," *Journal of Palestine Studies* 25, no. 3 (Spring 1996), pp. 93–100.

27 Ibid.

28 PNA, *1998 Third Quarter Donor Report*, chart 9.

29 Diwan and Shaban, *Development Under Adversity*, p. 32.

30 Mark, "Palestinians: U.S. Assistance to Palestinians," p. 9. The restrictive laws as of that date (that is, excluding the 1995 act) are detailed on pp. 10–11.

31 Ibid., pp. 3–4. Sara Roy, "U.S. Economic Aid to the West Bank and Gaza," p. 68, cites USAID documents showing a $5 million 1994 direct contribution to the PA police.

32 White House regular press briefing, September 29, 1998.

33 Secretary of State Albright at press conference on November 30, 1998; Walter Pincus, "White House, Congress Find Wye Pact Funds After Battle," *Washington Post*, December 12, 1998, p. A29.

34 "Jordan: U.S. Relations and Bilateral Issues" (Washington: Congressional Research Service, June 16, 1993), p. 11. See Alba Amawi, "USAID in Jordan," *Middle East Policy* 4, no. 4 (Spring 1996), pp. 77–89.

35 At his press conference on October 1, 1993, with Crown Prince Hassan of Jordan and Foreign Minister Peres of Israel—well before the signing of the Jordan–Israel peace treaty—President Clinton said, "There needs to be some debt relief for Jordan, and the United States will support that." See P.V. Vivekanand, "U.S. to write off $696 million in Jordan's debts," *Jordan Times*, July 30, 1994, p. 1.

36   Remarks by President Clinton to the Jordanian parliament, White House Office of the Press Secretary, October 26, 1994.

37   Letter to authors from Max Dupuy, U.S. Treasury Department, Office of Middle Eastern, Central Asian, and South Asian Nations, December 4, 1998.

38   Eric Stijger, "*Peace Falcon* over Jordan," *Code One* (October 1998), pp. 2–7.

39   On the aid transfer issue, see Martin Seiff, "Moving Cash to Jordan Mulled," *Washington Times*, May 16, 1997, p. A15; "U.S. Gives More Aid to Jordan," Associated Press, June 17, 1997; and Patrick Worsnip, "U.S. Announces $100 Million More Aid to Jordan," Reuters, June 17, 1997.

40   Clyde Mark, "Middle East and North Africa: Table Comparing U.S. Foreign Aid, FY1997, FY1998, and Requested FY1999," *CRS Report for Congress*, April 20, 1998, pp. 1–2.

41   Ibid.; Thomas Lippman, "Clinton to Sign Aid Bill Containing a Reward for Jordan," *Washington Post*, November 26, 1997, p. 22; and information from the State Department's Jordan desk.

42   This issue, raised in interviews with Jordanian officials, is rarely discussed in print, but see Chris Hedges, "As PLO Replaces Israelis, Jordan Remains on Sideline," *New York Times*, May 29, 1994, p. 12; and Ze'ev Schiff, "No Euphoria in Jordan," *Ha'aretz*, July 24, 1995, p. B1, as translated and printed in Joint Publication Research Service–Near East, JPRS-NEA 94-045, August 18, 1994, p. 34. For a fuller technical discussion, see Arie Arnon et al., *The Palestinian Economy* (Leiden, Netherlands: Brill, 1997), pp. 138–164.

43   The lower estimate comes from interviews at the Central Bank of Jordan. The higher estimate comes from World Bank, *Peace and the Jordanian Economy* (Washington: World Bank, 1994), as cited in Arnon et al., *The Palestinian Economy*, p. 153. The latter source also estimated that $1 billion in Israeli shekels was held in the territories.

44   Pincus, "White House, Congress Find Wye Pact Funds After Battle"; Francesca Ciriaci, "Albright stresses Jordan's 'involvement' in final status issues," *Jordan Times* online edition, December 17, 1998, at http://www.access2arabia.com/jordantimes/.

45   Richard Lawless, "Lebanon: Economy," *The Middle East and North Africa 1998* (London: Europa, 1998), pp. 728–729.

46   USAID, "Lebanon Program Background and Description," September 1998; and USAID Congressional Presentation, "Lebanon," n.d. [1998].

47   Mark, "Middle East and North Africa: Table Comparing U.S. Foreign Aid," p. 4.

48   Dana Priest, "U.S. is Lebanese Army's Patron,"*Washington Post*, December 5, 1998, p. A18.

49   U.S. Department of State, *Patterns of Global Terrorism 1997* (Washington: Government Printing Office, 1998), p. 34.

50 David Butter, "Syria Turns Over a New Leaf," *MEED*, September 5, 1997, p. 4.

51 David Butter, "Syria Reaps Rewards of Regional Policies," *MEED*, September 27, 1991, pp. 4–5.

52 Butter, "Syria Turns Over a New Leaf," pp. 4–5.

53 David Bucan, "MEPs Block Aid to Syria and Morocco," *Financial Times*, January 16, 1992.

54 A detailed analysis of the reasons why is provided by Fred Lawson, "Can U.S. Economic Assistance Alter Syria's Posture toward Israel?," *Middle East Policy* 4, no. 4 (Summer 1996), pp. 102–109.

55 Itamar Rabinovich, *The Brink of Peace* (Princeton, N.J.: Princeton University Press, 1998), p. 225. The phrase "as a bridge," which the context suggests may be the phrase of then–Secretary of State Warren Christopher, is on p. 216.

Chapter 3

Aid to Israel and Egypt

U.S. aid to the newer participants in the peace process is frequently compared to the aid received by Israel and Egypt after they signed the Camp David accords and became the first countries in the Levant to accept peace. But in the 1970s and early 1980s, Washington was much more generous with its aid packages; the context for the aid debate in the 1990s and the coming decade is entirely different from that of the Camp David era. Currently, there is a strong mood in Washington against aid in general. This mood is partly a product of the tight federal government budgetary situation, but there is also much skepticism about the extent to which aid helped the poor. Conservatives are suspicious that aid reinforces inefficient governments at the expense of markets, and liberals tend to wonder if aid ends up benefiting the powerful without doing much for the disenfranchised. As a result, the U.S. budget for international development and humanitarian assistance has changed little since the mid-1980s, at constant prices. At the same time, the end of the Cold War has led to a considerable reduction in the U.S. budget for international security assistance.

Given these tighter financial constraints, therefore, an important question about aid and the peace process is, What leverage over the recipients do aid flows give the United States? If the United States wishes to pressure the peace process partners—a question about which there has been vigorous domestic U.S. debate—then it needs to have effective instruments for applying pressure. Many such instruments have been discussed, such as publicly expressed disapproval and United Nations Security Council votes. The question here is whether threats to change the aid flows are credible and effective, and the answer can be found by reviewing Washington's history of providing aid packages to Egypt and Israel. Particularly worth examining is the 1992 dispute with Israel over loan guarantees: Did this dispute materially affect Israel's peace process stance? If so, what made economic pressure effective in this case, and why has it not been used in other situations?

In light of the tight resource constraints and doubts about the utility of aid, the lessons of history—specifically, the history of U.S. aid to Israel and Egypt—should be studied to learn what has worked best and what has encountered serious problems.

ISRAEL

Two major changes in the program of U.S. aid to Israel took place in the 1990s: the loan guarantee program approved in 1992 and the phase-out of economic aid combined with a one-time, post–Wye River Memorandum allocation in 1998–1999. These changes could not have better captured the issue of how much influence over Israel the U.S. government receives by giving the country aid. The loan guarantee dispute saw a national debate in Israel about policies to which the United States was objecting, with the U.S. stance arguably influencing a national election. By contrast, the economic aid phase-out suggests that aid is becoming a less potent tool of U.S. policy for advancing the peace process.

Background

The United States provided aid to Israel only on a small scale until 1971, when Israel found itself confronting Arab armies supplied with the most modern Soviet armaments.[1] The United States recognized the strategic importance of supporting a small ally that could not match with its own resources the flow of advanced weaponry the Soviets were supplying the Arab states. Providing Israel with military aid was a way to drain the Soviets, whose economy could ill-afford the race to produce ever-more-sophisticated weaponry. In addition, the Israelis battle-tested U.S. equipment against the best the Soviets had. During the course of the Cold War, most of the Soviet-built weaponry destroyed in battle was destroyed by Israel.

In addition to military aid, the United States started to provide substantial cash economic assistance in 1975 (in 1967–1974, total economic aid was $156 million). Yet, in many ways, even that cash assistance was simply another form of military aid, this time paying for past military purchases. As its military purchases from the United States grew sharply, Israel started borrowing large sums: $2.1 billion total from 1971 through 1974 (equivalent to $8.2 billion at 1998 prices), which was equivalent to

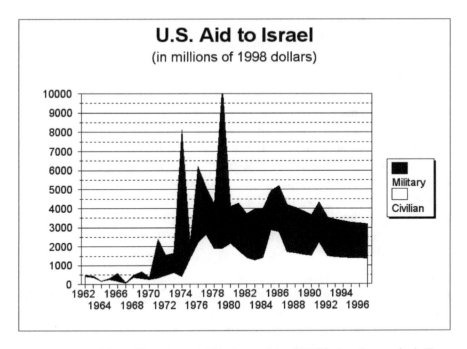

U.S. Aid to Israel
(in millions of 1998 dollars)

6.8 percent of Israel's gross national product (GNP) for the period. Furthermore, by the mid-1970s and especially after the weighty 1973 October War, it was clear that Israel's large-scale weapons purchases were going to be an ongoing requirement, not just a one-time occurrence. Whereas it is sound economic policy to finance a one-time war-cost with debt, this is much less the case for military spending that will be required every year for the foreseeable future. It was in this context that the U.S. cash economic assistance program began. In other words, the cash aid program, even after Camp David, was not necessarily linked to the peace process with Egypt. To be sure, Israel's withdrawal from Sinai added another argument for cash aid, both to reward Israel and to help it offset the costs incurred replacing the military assets, like airbases, in the territory from which it was withdrawing.

When Israel faced an extreme economic crisis in 1985–1986, the United States stepped in with supplemental cash aid. Thereafter, the aid flow leveled off at $1.8 billion a year in military aid and $1.2 billion a year in economic aid. The main factor determining the level of economic aid was that this was the amount needed to cover Israel's debt payments for the loan component of the aid prior to 1986. Indeed, the debt had to be restructured and stretched out to keep payments each year below the level of economic aid. Israel also received small amounts of directed aid for such purposes as resettling refugees (originally, in large part, those from the Soviet Union) and supporting American-sponsored schools and hospitals in Israel.

When the $3-billion-a-year aid program began, it was essential to Israel's well-being. In 1985, U.S. aid was equal to 12 percent of Israel's GNP. As Israel put its economic house in order, U.S. aid became less important: The economy grew in an export-led boom, while the aid remained fixed (its real value fell with inflation). By 1991, the aid was equal to only 6 percent of the country's GNP, and in 1998, the aid package was equal to only 3 percent of GNP. What once had been essential had become much less important economically. At the same time, the aid had become a symbol of how strong the security relationship is between the United States and Israel. It is in that context that the loan guarantee dispute of 1991–1992 played out.

Loan Guarantee Dispute. The single most prominent example of using economics to promote the diplomatic agenda of the peace process was the loan guarantee dispute of 1991–1992. The issue of U.S. loan guarantees to Israel arose during the 1991 Gulf War as a conjunction of two interests: The United States was eager to encourage Israel to stay out of the conflict despite the missiles falling on Tel Aviv, and Israel faced serious economic problems caused by lost production during the war (when much economic activity came to a halt) as well as by the need to absorb the 20,000 immigrants arriving each month from the former Soviet Union and Ethiopia. In March, as the war ended, the Bush administration agreed to an Israeli request for $650 million in war-cost aid, on the condition that any request for immigrant absorption aid be postponed to September—both so that the aid could come out of the next fiscal year's budget and so that the United States would not be making a new major commitment to Israel at the same time that Secretary of State James Baker was arranging a regional peace conference.[2] There was a clear expectation that Israel would get additional aid, both to reward it for staying out of the war and to help it absorb immigrants; the issue was only the timing. So whereas it is true that the subsequent debate was about whether Israel would get additional aid (not whether the existing aid flow would be cut), it is also fair to say that Israel expected the aid on the basis of statements made during the war—statements that were a factor in Israel's decision not to retaliate against the missile strikes.

Baker devoted the summer of 1991 to shuttling to the Middle East to set up a regional conference, but he had not tied up all the loose ends by September, so President George Bush mounted an all-out lobbying effort to persuade Israel to defer for 120 days the aid request, which had been pared back to a loan guarantee—not even a loan, much less a grant.[3] Saying the potential for Middle East peace was at stake, Bush played political hard-ball, implying at a press conference that he was taking a politically courageous stance against the pro-Israel lobby:

> I'm up against some powerful political forces . . . I heard today that there were something like a thousand lobbyists on the Hill working the other side of the question. We've got one lonely little guy down here doing it . . . I don't care if I get one [only] vote, I'm going to stand for what I believe here . . . And if necessary, I will use my veto power.[4]

Bush won his point: The aid request was delayed for the four months he requested. During that time, the Madrid peace conference was held, launching direct talks between Israel and its Arab neighbors to the north and east—Lebanon, Syria, Jordan, and the Palestinians (theoretically as part of the Jordanian delegation). Although analysts and participants are divided about whether the delayed aid request made a material difference in the convening of the Madrid peace conference, the Bush administration thought the delay was important for the peace process, and Washington successfully applied pressure to delay providing what Israel thought it had been promised.

In January 1992, the loan guarantee request got hung up by a new issue: Bush's strong opposition to Israeli settlements in the West Bank and Gaza.[5] After a month of debate with the Israeli government about the guarantees, Baker publicly tied the two issues together, proclaiming, "This administration is ready to support loan guarantees for absorption assistance to Israel of up to $2 billion a year for five years, provided, though, there is a halt or end to settlement activity."[6] Senator Patrick Leahy (D-Vt.) proposed the compromise that was eventually adopted in September 1992, namely, to deduct from the loan guarantees an amount equal to what Israel spends on the settlements.[7] Yet, the compromise was reached only after a bitter debate.

The Bush administration's approach was to put maximum pressure on Israeli prime minister Yitzhak Shamir to change a policy Shamir saw as vital for Israel—namely, building settlements in the West Bank and Gaza. It seems unlikely that the administration thought Shamir would be flexible, given his strong sentiments on the matter. Part of Washington's calculation was that Israel was heading for elections on June 23, 1992, and opposition leader Yitzhak Rabin's position was closer to that of the United

States. Rabin assured, "We will halt political settlements out of Israeli considerations whether it is linked to a loan from the U.S. or not," though he added the weak caveat, "It is *desirable* [emphasis added] that no foreign element get involved in any internal matter of the state of Israel."[8] The issue escalated into a real crisis in the minds of Israelis; relations with the United States were seen as a turning point. When Rabin won the election, the Bush approach looked like the real winner: The United States had effectively used the aid issue to achieve a change in an Israeli policy to which every administration since Lyndon Johnson had objected.

Yet, the Bush approach had several downsides. First, the U.S. opposition to settlements encouraged the Shamir government to rush to build settlements. Arguably, had Bush not opposed the settlements so adamantly, the Shamir government would have built less housing in the West Bank and Gaza. Second, the Bush approach was high-stakes poker. Suppose the election results had been different—a plausible outcome, given that Rabin's coalition had a narrow margin of victory. Then the United States would almost certainly not have provided the loan guarantees, and Shamir would almost certainly have dug in his heels on holding on to the West Bank and Gaza. Quite possibly, there would have been a noticeable cooling in U.S.–Israel relations.

The paradox about the loan guarantee dispute is that the economic need for the guarantees was never particularly clear; the $10 billion figure was selected for political reasons during the Gulf War, rather than being the product of economic analysis. The justification for that figure evaporated as immigration to Israel tapered off (from 20,000 a month in early 1991 to 5,000 a month by mid-1992) and the Israeli economy took off. In the midst of the dispute, former Israeli state budget director David Boaz argued that the loan guarantees were not needed and that they would create an "easy money" atmosphere in which needed reforms would be delayed and the money wasted.[9] During the loan guarantee debate, a variety of voices across the political spectrum, from the hawkish to the liberal, spoke out in favor of reducing or phasing out U.S. aid altogether.[10] In the end, Israel borrowed the funds primarily because it perceived that it would have been politically unwise not to take advantage of the loan guarantees it had fought so hard to obtain.

A further irony is that, in the end, the U.S. government took a relaxed attitude about Israeli expenditures in the West Bank and Gaza. Whereas the United States calculated that $1,359 million was spent on investments in the territories, it classified $585 million as necessary security expenditures, such as to build roads bypassing Arab villages. The reduction from the amount made available under the loan guarantee program was $774 million, with the reductions in 1996 and 1997 being only $60 million a year.

Whether the loan guarantees were economically needed was never the point, but Israeli public opinion became fixated on the issue. The dispute raised the question of how close and abiding was the U.S.–Israel relationship. In other words, the loan guarantee dispute showed that the United States could (and can) use economic aid as an instrument to cause Israelis to reflect on what they must do to keep the bilateral relationship strong.

Phasing Out Aid. Fast-forwarding to 1998, the issue of aid changed 180 degrees from whether Israel needed more aid to whether Israel could do without aid. In the interim, Israel experienced five years of rapid growth that raised per capita income from $10,000 in 1989 to $16,000 in 1995—60 percent of U.S. income—at which level it stabilized in 1996–1998. Israel's per capita income puts it solidly in the midst of the developed countries, ahead of several European states (Greece, Ireland, Portugal, and Spain). Furthermore, Israel's debt payments to the United States had begun to decline. In the past, the entire $1.2 billion in economic aid was earmarked for debt payments, with nothing left over to finance Israeli expenditures. From the late 1990s, it will be possible to reduce aid yet maintain that same system—that is, economic aid will go toward debt payment with nothing left over. Bearing in mind these realities, Israeli prime minister Binyamin Netanyahu pledged in a July 1996 address to the U.S. Congress, "In the next four years we are going to begin the long-term process of gradually reducing the level of your generous economic assistance to Israel." [11]

Indeed, in spring 1998, Finance Minister Ya'akov Ne'eman suggested phasing out the $1.2 billion in economic aid over ten to twelve years, with half the savings being applied to increase military aid; the expectation was that the other half would be used for other Middle East aid, especially for Jordan.[12] The reduction would be phased to maintain sufficient funds each year to pay for Israel's debt service; in later years, the principal due would be prepaid until, in the last year, the debt would be fully repaid. In the United States, discussions on the aid package were protracted. The Clinton administration and some in Congress wanted faster and deeper cuts, with a reduction of $150 million a year during each of the first three years and only one-third transferred to military aid.[13] There was also debate over whether Israel could use the additional military aid to pay for defense purchases made in Israel rather than in America.[14] In the end, the fiscal year (FY) 1999 budget included a $120 million reduction in economic aid along with a $60

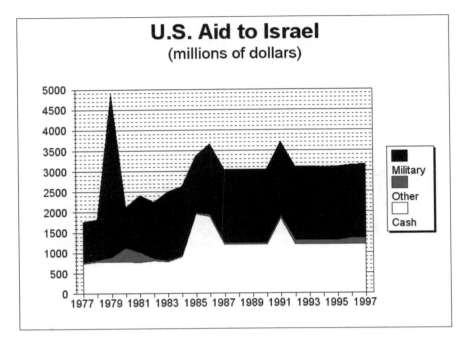

U.S. Aid to Israel
(millions of dollars)

million increase in military aid. The aid levels in future years will be determined by Congress only when those years arrive, but it does seem likely that the economic aid to Israel will be phased out over the next decade.

Paradoxically, at the same time as Israel has suggested that the United States phase out economic aid, it has also proposed that Washington provide a new aid package of $1.2 billion, this time to facilitate Israeli withdrawal from part of the West Bank. Moreover, it would seem that the United States agreed to the full amount that Israel requested.[15] This new aid package would pay for several projects, such as to improve Israel's counterterrorism capabilities and to modernize or replace Israel's aging airborne-intelligence-gathering planes and its attack helicopters, which are used against tanks as well as against terrorists. These expenditures are not necessarily directly related to the Wye-mandated withdrawals, but they will make Israel more secure against the threats that opponents of withdrawal emphasize—terrorism from PA-controlled areas and the risk that future instability in Jordan will allow Iraqi armor to advance through Jordan into the West Bank.

The expenses more directly associated with the Wye withdrawals will be only a fraction of the $1.2 billion. The redeployment plan prepared by the Israel Defense Forces entails relocating from the West Bank the main training camps used by the two Israeli elite brigades (the Golani brigade and the paratrooper brigade) and arms depots with thousands of heavy weapons used by reserve units. A more controversial project would involve building bypass roads to allow Israeli settlers to travel without having to go through areas under PA control. Bypass roads would reduce the chances of a violent incident and so would seem a natural means to reinforce the Wye River accord. The problem arises as to where the new roads would go, because it is unlikely that Israel would, in the final status agreement, hand back the area where the roads go. Moreover, building the roads requires taking land from Palestinians, which engenders ill will.

Policy Issues

Aid was important in solidifying support for the Camp David accords, both as a symbol of the U.S. commitment and because of the resources provided, which facilitated the multibillion-dollar construction of military facilities to make up for those in the Sinai. Yet, in many ways, the changed situation today makes aid less important to Israel's attitudes toward peace:

- The strategic ties with the United States have deepened over the last twenty years, reducing the U.S. need to provide a concrete embodiment of that relationship, in terms of traditional economic assistance.

- Israel's conventional strategic situation is generally much better, in that its potential enemies do not have the support of a superpower; Israel is no longer locked into an arms race with opponents who have access to an endless supply of ever-improving advanced weapons.

- Israel's economic situation is much better, such that the country is better-positioned to absorb post–peace treaty transitional redeployment costs.

Israeli attitudes toward the peace treaty with Jordan and the Oslo accords did not seem to be influenced by the absence of additional U.S. aid, though it is not clear if this will be the case with regard to the Wye River agreement. As Israel redeploys from additional areas in the West Bank, it will require large expenditures to replace training camps and arms depots and to build roads to provide security for settlers. Partly for that reason, the one-time $1.2 billion in U.S. aid planned for 1999 to offset that agreement's costs may have some influence on Israeli attitudes toward the Wye agreement. Even if aid would make only a small difference in the Israeli debate about redeployments and final status, that small difference may be sufficient to tip scales that might otherwise be in balance between two opposing camps.

Israeli–Syrian peace, if it includes significant withdrawal from the Golan Heights, could resurrect the aid-for-peace issue on terms more like those seen after Camp David. Redeployment of Israeli forces stationed on the Golan will be expensive, as will replacing the early-warning and intelligence assets located on the Golan, especially if that requires space-based intelligence and early-warning systems. Furthermore, many Israelis could be wavering about the benefits of peace with Syria, but their attitudes could be significantly improved were the United States to finance the new Israeli military assets needed to replace what the IDF would lose by withdrawing from the Golan Heights. Indeed, support for a treaty with Syria could be influenced positively were the Israeli government able to package it with a major program to upgrade Israel's military equipment. Such a program could include precision-strike weaponry guided by tightly interlinked command-and-control technology interacting with advanced sensors, thus bringing Israel more fully in line with the revolution in military affairs (RMA) that is transforming how the U.S. military operates. In other words, a multibillion-dollar military modernization program, with substantial U.S. support, could make an appreciable difference in how comfortable Israelis feel about withdrawal from the Golan. Not that such aid would be the only factor, nor necessarily the decisive factor, in any decision about Golan withdrawal, but it could make a difference.

A rather different issue is whether threats to *withhold* aid could promote a more helpful Israeli stance on peace process issues. The possibility that senior U.S. officials would consider this option cannot be excluded. The loan guarantee dispute showed how a high-profile confrontation with the United States over economic aid can influence Israeli attitudes. The Israeli public values highly its strategic relationship with the United States and does not want to see it put at risk. Moreover, the pressure may itself be counterproductive: It could create a backlash, a stubborn reaction against foreigners perceived as putting Israel's security at risk. At most, this policy could produce a short-term gain but at a long-term risk.

In general, the phasing out of the economic aid program will substantially reduce the potential for Washington to use aid as an instrument of leverage. At the same time, the economic aid program's phase-out will create opportunities for Washington to provide more aid to other Middle East peace process parties, given the zero-sum realities of U.S. budget limits on overall aid. There have been many claims on the funds made available by the reduction in Israeli aid, and the experience of 1997–1998 is that there will be a vigorous discussion about what use of those funds will best advance the peace process. That is a subject on which the Israeli government is sure to express its opinion, as is fit and proper. At the same time, the United States has an interest in firmly establishing the principle that the allocation of such money is up to the U.S. government to decide; the funds are not Israel's to reprogram. After all, it is possible that the United States will determine that the best use of the funds may not be in the Middle East: There are other pressing U.S. interests besides the promotion of the Arab–Israeli peace process. It would be unfortunate if the 1997–1998 experience were to create the impression that Middle Easterners have a permanent claim on U.S. resources and that any funds made available through a reduction in aid to some peace process countries have to be redirected to other peace process purposes.

EGYPT

Since the mid-1980s, U.S. aid committed to Egypt has been pegged at $2 billion a year, of which $1.2 billion is military assistance and $0.8 billion is economic aid. This assistance is less like U.S. aid to Israel and more like the aid America provides to other international recipients, in that it takes the form of financing for reform efforts and for projects; actual disbursement in any year therefore depends on the pace at which the reforms and projects proceed. Nevertheless, in the minds of all parties, American and Middle Eastern, a strong link has existed between the level of aid to Egypt and to Israel; therefore, as aid to Israel is reduced, aid to Egypt will also likely decline. The question is how to change the aid without adversely affecting the peace process or U.S.–Egyptian relations.

Background

The United States has long been a major aid provider to Egypt. During several periods when political relations were not particularly close, the United States nevertheless provided substantial humanitarian assistance in the form of food aid, which ranged from around $200 million annually in the mid-1970s to a peak of $300 million annually in the early 1980s. This program was phased out after 1985, and the last substantial disbursement was made in 1991. In addition to food aid, the United States began its project aid in the early 1970s at the invitation of Egyptian president Anwar Sadat. The U.S. aid program was motivated by the strategic environment of the mid-1970s in which Soviet allies were coming to power in several African countries—such as Angola and Ethiopia—and the oil-producing countries were flexing their economic muscles.

Prior to 1978—the date of the Camp David accords—U.S. project aid to Egypt primarily took the form of loans for infrastructure projects. In

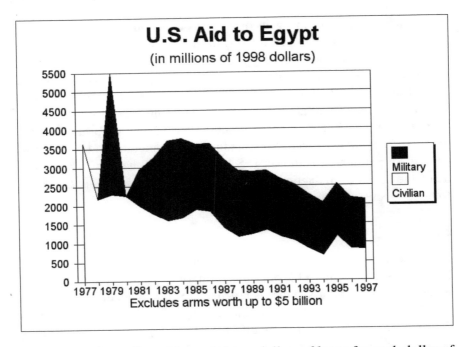

U.S. Aid to Egypt
(in millions of 1998 dollars)

Military

Civilian

1977 1979 1981 1983 1985 1987 1989 1991 1993 1995 1997

Excludes arms worth up to $5 billion

1979 and 1980, project aid equaled two dollars of loans for each dollar of grants; from 1982 on, project aid has consisted entirely of grants, as has the cash aid program that was then instituted to support economic reforms. As for military aid, that began after Camp David in 1979 with a $1.5 billion loan to replace Soviet equipment with Western arms. Washington lent a further $3 billion in 1981–1984, and a grant program began in 1982. The combined level of military aid to Egypt, in both loans and grants, has averaged $1.3 billion a year since 1983, with loans being part of the package only in the first two years. In sum, Camp David was a turning point not only in the volume of aid but also in its composition, which shifted quickly from humanitarian aid and project loans to grants for military equipment, economic reforms, and infrastructure projects.

The post–Camp David aid came at an opportune time for Egypt. The accords with Israel had resulted in Egypt's ostracism by other Arab governments at a time when the oil producers were flush with cash and were dispensing considerable amounts of aid. Furthermore, Egypt's economy was a mess. Afraid of political unrest if he too quickly removed subsidies and shed excess employees in state enterprises, Sadat kept the economy burdened with much of the Nasserist heritage of controls, despite his rhetorical commitment to opening to a market economy. As a result, the balance of payments was hemorrhaging, forcing Egypt to a level of borrowing that drove the country's foreign debt up from $7 billion in 1976 to $21 billion in 1980 (admittedly, $6 billion of that $14 billion increase was because of aid-linked loans from the U.S.). In this context, Egypt could use any help it could get, and the U.S. aid was massive relative to the size of the economy: It averaged 8 percent of the GNP each year during the first decade after Sadat's 1977 trip to Jerusalem.

The military component of the aid financed the purchase of advanced Western armaments for the Egyptian military. At a time when the military was becoming less politically prominent as the byproduct of the peace with Israel, these Western armaments could only help the morale of an Egyptian military pampered from years of receiving ample advanced armaments from the Soviet Union. Over and above its impact on the peace process, the military aid also served U.S. interests by making the Egyptian military interoperable with U.S. forces in the event of troubles in the Persian Gulf, which was then in the throes of the Iranian Revolution and soon the Iran–Iraq War. In short, U.S. aid was an effective "peace bribe," providing an inducement to keep the peace treaty alive during moments of stress like the 1982 Israeli invasion of Lebanon.

By the late 1990s, much has changed in ways that make the aid less important:

- The economy is doing well, with no net foreign debt (foreign debt is less than foreign reserves, a situation helped by Washington's Gulf War write-off of $6.7 billion of Egypt's military debt), 6 percent annual real growth, and per capita income ($1,180 in 1997) high enough to put Egypt in the World Bank's middle-income category. The government is actually implementing a broad array of economic reforms.

- Politically, the peace treaty is accepted as being advantageous; very few Egyptians want to return to the days of confrontation and danger of war. Egypt is a leader in the Arab world, with little criticism of its peace with Israel. Cairo faced the Arab world squarely in the eye over its peace treaty and forced the latter to blink. Although one can justly criticize the coolness of Egypt–Israel peace, Cairo kept its promise not to buckle to Arab criticism, sanctions, or ostracism; Egypt's peace with Israel is a fact of life that all other Arab leaders now accept.

- The military has limited need for new equipment. Its stocks of advanced Western arms exceed what it has been able to absorb, and its soldiers do not make effective use of the material now on hand. Only selected items, such as a system to defend against missiles, are clearly urgent.

The aid program consists of two major components: economic aid and military aid. The civilian aid in turn is composed of three major elements: cash assistance, the commodity import program, and development project aid.

Economic Aid. Economic aid to Egypt has been motivated by more than just the peace process. Economic aid has done much to launch Egypt on a path of sustainable economic development. Indeed, the economic aid program has had two major successes: rebuilding the physical infrastructure and encouraging structural reforms. Especially in its first decade, economic aid financed the renovation and expansion of the decrepit and overstretched physical infrastructure. In its second decade, economic aid encouraged policy reforms that have launched Egypt on a path of sustainable growth. This has had an important demonstration effect on other Arab countries, encouraging reform throughout the region.

The three major components of the aid program are cash assistance, the commodity import program, and development project aid. Cash assistance, $265 million of which was allocated for FY1999, has been effective at promoting economic reform by tying cash payouts to reform measures. The commodity import program, which Congress has for years mandated at $200 million a year, now finances Egyptian private sector imports of U.S. equipment and material. Development project aid is about $350 million a year, of which about $125 million goes for electricity and telecommunications and $87 million for sewers and air pollution abatement. The FY1999 budget includes $109 million for population and health, non-infrastructure environment, democracy, and education. There are also programs, with large shares allocated to U.S. consultants, to support privatization, small enterprise credit, and private sector exports.

In the late 1990s, pressure began to build to reduce the aid program to Egypt, motivated by a variety of factors: pressures on the U.S. budget, the perception that the program was less vital to U.S. interests than it had once been, and the desire to find resources to fund aid for Jordan. In FY1997 and FY1998, aid to Egypt was reduced by cutting down the pipeline of undisbursed funds by $66 million the first year and $50 million the second. The Egyptian government was none too pleased by these developments, but it did not object strenuously for several reasons: The pipeline reduction was unlikely to have much effect on aid disbursements for years to come, the reduction went to fund aid to a fellow Arab country which thus felt a certain gratitude to Egypt (though this should not be exagger-

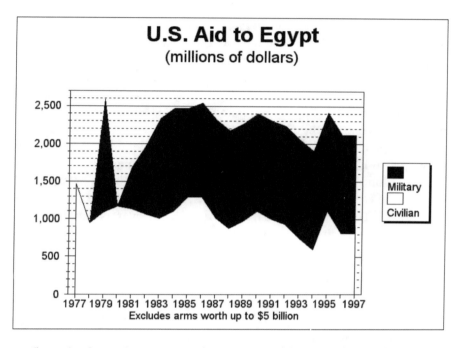

U.S. Aid to Egypt
(millions of dollars)

2,500

2,000

1,500
Military

1,000
Civilian

500

0
1977 1979 1981 1983 1985 1987 1989 1991 1993 1995 1997
Excludes arms worth up to $5 billion

ated), and—far and away most important—aid to Israel was also cut by $50 million each year. As consideration of the FY1999 budget began, the outlook for Egypt aid was transformed by the Israeli proposal to phase out economic aid to that country over ten to twelve years, with half the money being added to military aid. In some initial maneuvering—motivated more by personality politics in Washington than by any Egyptian lobbying— some in Congress proposed an identical program for Egyptian aid—that is, a 10 percent reduction in economic aid with half the money added to military aid. In the end, however, economic aid to Egypt was cut to $775 million, a reduction of $40 million (about 5 percent), while military aid was left unchanged. The House Appropriations Committee report stated it "believes this forms the basis for similar annual decreases of $40,000,000 over a period of not more than ten years which will result in a 50 percent reduction in economic assistance to Egypt."[16] In a move vaguely analo- gous to cutting Israel's usual economic aid 10 percent and then dedicating 5 percent to a new purpose, the Senate Appropriations Committee report said that Egypt's economic aid should be cut $40 million and an additional $40 million from the aid should be "made available to Egypt to establish an Enterprise Fund" to "strengthen private sector development" and to "shift away from large project support."[17]

Military Aid. At first, U.S. military assistance to Egypt was a reward for making peace with Israel and so was tied to U.S. aid levels to Israel. Over time, however, the U.S.–Egypt strategic partnership assumed an importance of its own. The result is that today, the U.S. relationship with Egypt, and particularly with Egypt's military, is a critical asset to U.S. interests for reasons largely unrelated to the peace process. The U.S. military presence in the Gulf and the region at large is dependent on a logistical pipeline that runs through Egypt. No matter how vocally Cairo may oppose U.S. diplomatic tactics or military planning—as it has repeatedly done vis-à-vis Iraq and the peace process—it has never failed to grant the United States overflight rights, basing, or transit through the Suez Canal. The political and strategic reality, however, is that decreases in U.S. assistance are sure to affect Egypt's willingness to cooperate so speedily and effectively.

Moreover, Egypt has committed troops on several occasions to support U.S. policy initiatives. Cairo sent forces to prop up the regime in Zaire in 1977, to help Morocco in the war against radical Algeria in 1979, to oppose Libyan operations in Sudan in 1983, to defend Saudi Arabia in 1990, to police Somalia in 1992, and to pacify Bosnia in 1994. In many of those interventions, Egyptian forces provided the politically critical element that allowed intervention by the United States and the West.

As mentioned earlier, military aid has been at $1.3 billion a year since 1983; by 1998, however, the real value of that aid had declined by one-third because of inflation. Nevertheless, Egypt has also been allocated $5 billion in excess military equipment, which averages out to about $250 million a year during the twenty years since Camp David. Most of that equipment was provided to Egypt during the large-scale drawdown of U.S. equipment after the Cold War. At 1998 prices, the military aid (including excess equipment) provided to Egypt since Camp David has been worth $35 billion. Yet, past aid-financed purchases are not being used particularly effectively. Little money is spent on operations and maintenance, and troops are unable to spend sufficient time training with equipment to be proficient in its use. Egypt devotes most of its limited military budget to salaries; numbers in the military are kept high for fear of exacerbating the country's unemployment problem. In other words, Egypt has acquired a lot of U.S.-paid-for equipment that it cannot use effectively. Refocusing the aid to address this problem would not be easy. The military aid has been programmed for years to come for new weapons, which would make politically difficult any quick moves to reorient it or to reduce it.

Policy Issues

The basic rationale for supporting Egypt and strengthening the strategic partnership remains unchanged—to cement Egypt–Israel peace, the cornerstone of all peacemaking efforts; to assist the Egyptian regime in its battle against religious extremism for the hearts and minds of the Egyptian people; and to secure Egypt as a positive model of a pro-West, pro-peace, status quo power to the states and peoples of the Arab and Islamic worlds.

Economic Aid. Despite its recent progress, Egypt still faces huge obstacles to growth, ranging from the nearly 1 million new entrants to the labor market each year to the slow pace of privatization and the still-suffocating power of the state bureaucracy. Egypt will continue to need substantial U.S. assistance to ensure the success of its reform effort, and the overall importance of the strategic partnership makes investing in Egypt's economic health a vital U.S. interest; moreover, ending the aid program would be seen as a slap in the face of an Arab ally when the peace process is best served by an Arab perception that the United States cares about the well-being of Arabs. Therefore, instead of phasing out Egypt's economic aid (as is being done to Israel's economic aid), Washington should trim down and refashion its aid program with an eye toward promoting Egyptian exports, making Egypt more attractive for foreign investors, and assisting Egypt's transition to a free-market economy—all goals that would strengthen the U.S.–Egypt partnership and advance U.S. interests. The specific steps would include the following:

- Phasing out new project commitments. Of the more than $200 million spent each year on electricity, telecommunications, sewers, and air pollution abatement, much of it could be replaced by foreign private financing as Egypt privatizes state enterprises and introduces more competition. Ending future project commitments could be used as part of the Egyptian government's ongoing effort to send foreign investors a strong political message about Egypt's economic maturity. Currently, there is a $1.6 billion "pipeline" of undisbursed development-project aid. This backlog is equal to 4.5 years of annual spending, meaning that even if no funds were committed to new projects, disbursements would continue at close to present levels for two to three years and then taper off for another four to five years.

- Sustaining the "commodity import program" (CIP). Although economists generally regard this program as an inefficient way to transfer cash to the Egyptian government—because of excessive paperwork and opportunities for corruption—U.S. suppliers like programs that make U.S. goods more competitive relative to European goods. Maintaining this program is thus a political necessity.

- Giving priority to cash transfers. Although much progress has been made on the reform program, much remains to be done, as illustrated by the failure to secure the release of $550 million in cash aid committed but not yet disbursed (that is, also in the "pipeline"). The Egyptian government arguably appreciates most the cash component of aid, if for no other reason than because less of it is diverted into meeting the extraordinarily detailed bureaucratic requirements of the U.S. aid program.

- Complementing the reduced aid with a program to enhance Egyptian exports. Some portion of the aid funding could be dedicated to export enhancement through such activities as providing bilateral research-and-development endowments, giving industrial investment funds to promote foreign investment, creating "qualified industrial zones" to join Egypt and other peace process states, supporting an export promotion agency, and financing educational and training programs with U.S. firms and industries. More important, however, would be providing Egyptian exports, such as textiles, easier access to the U.S. market. As the restrictions on Egyptian exports were eliminated, it would become increasingly easier for the United States to start negotiatiations on a U.S.–Egypt free trade agreement.

Military Aid. As noted earlier, military aid to Egypt serves a variety of strategic purposes, only some of which are related to the Arab–Israeli peace process. Egypt is also part of the U.S. strategy for the Persian Gulf—not because Egypt would provide militarily significant forces to any U.S.-led operation in the Gulf, but because Egyptian forces would be politically essential for demonstrating Arab support for such an operation. Furthermore, access to Egyptian airspace is vital for planes flying from the United States or Europe to the Gulf. So a variety of reasons point to the need to sustain military aid to Egypt, even if such aid has little positive impact on the peace process.

Indeed, U.S. military aid to Egypt has had only a mixed, if somewhat positive, influence on the peace process. On the positive side, Egypt's strict implementation of the military aspects of the peace treaty with Israel, along with its record of operational support for U.S. initiatives, make a strong case that the aid has made the Egyptian military more accepting of peace and more willing to work with the United States. In fact, the Egyptian armed forces are among the most influential constituencies supporting peace with Israel. On the negative side, the aid has signaled Washington's support for Egypt on broad strategic grounds irrespective of differences on the peace process, and the aid has increased Egypt's military strength. These factors may have made Egypt more confident that it could act in ways that do not well-serve the peace process—maintaining a "cold peace" and competitive approach toward Israel, cozying up to rogue regimes in Libya and Sudan that at times support those who undermine the peace process, and publicly criticizing U.S. peace process initiatives.

Discussion of military aid to Egypt cannot be divorced from the Israel connection and an assessment of the dangers of "cold peace." To be sure, a number of safeguards exist to protect Israel from a direct risk being posed by the Egyptian forces:

- The two U.S. battalions stationed in the Sinai as part of the Multilateral Force and Observers (MFO) set up to support the Egypt–Israel peace treaty play a crucial role. The "cold peace" highlights the continuing importance of that peacekeeping force.

- The heavy dependence of the Egyptian military on U.S. logistical support is insurance against an Egyptian return to confrontation with Israel. Former Washington Institute fellow Kenneth Pollack has found compelling evidence that, in 1995, Cairo wanted to conduct a squadron-sized air-strike against Khartoum to retaliate for Sudan's complicity in the assassination attempt against Egyptian president Husni Mubarak earlier that year. Yet, when Washington forbade U.S. military personnel from assisting with the operation, Cairo was forced to call off the attack because the Egyptians could not themselves handle its logistical requirements.

- Despite the efforts of thousands of U.S. advisers and billions of new weapons, Egypt's military capabilities have progressed only modestly over the last twenty-five years and almost certainly have not kept pace with improvements in Israeli capabilities. Indicators such as Egypt's mediocre performance in the Gulf War suggest that the Egyptian army would likely fare worse against Israel today than it did in October 1973.

- Egypt's forces would require immediate, constant and massive resupply in the event of conflict. In 1973—when Egypt's forces were at their logistical peak—Cairo acquired aid from the Soviets to sustain its war against Israel. Today, such resupply would be even more essential because Cairo has allowed its stockpiles of munitions and spare parts to dwindle, but Egypt knows that it would never receive U.S. support in a battle with Israel.

Despite all these safeguards, Israelis continue to be worried about Egyptian armaments. The principal reason for concern is their sense that many, if not most, Egyptians have still not reconciled themselves to Israel's right to statehood and tolerate the peace treaty only because of the latter's military strength; change the balance and peace would dissolve.

Against this background, any increase in the dollar amount of military aid would send the wrong political and strategic message. At the same time, a decrease in military aid to Egypt, concurrent with plans for a sizable (that is, $600-million-a-year) boost in military aid to Israel, is likely to inject political strain into the U.S.–Egypt military relationship and unnecessarily complicate the strategic relationship between Washington and Cairo. Staying the course on military aid, therefore, is the appropriate policy.

But that alone will not solve the problem of a deepening freeze in the Egypt–Israel military relationship. Whereas this is just one aspect of the "cold peace," it is one with potentially strategic consequences. As a result, it deserves higher priority on Washington's crowded Middle East agenda. Reversing the downward trend in Israel–Egypt relations, especially through military-to-military ties, is an important U.S. interest. The new U.S.–Egypt "strategic dialogue" may provide a useful vehicle to address this problem, but its solution can clearly be found only through America's continued deep engagement with the Egyptian military.

NOTES

1 U.S. aid to Israel from 1949 through 1970 averaged $376 million a year at 1998 prices.

2 Thomas Friedman, "U.S. to Give Israel $650 Million To Offset Its Costs in Gulf War," *New York Times*, March 6, 1991, pp. A1, A16.

3 John Goshko and John Yang, "Bush Asks 4-Month Delay On Israeli Housing Aid," *Washington Post*, September 7, 1991, p. A12.

4 "Excerpts from Bush's Comments: We Must Avoid a Contentious Debate," *New York Times*, September 13, 1991, p. A10.

5 John Goshko, "Pared-Down Loan Guarantee Plan Is Likely to Be Offered to Israel," *Washington Post*, January 23, 1992, p. A15.

6   John Goshko, "Baker Bars Israeli Loan Aid Unless Settlements Are Halted," *Washington Post*, February 25, 1992, pp. A1 and A14.

7   Thomas Friedman, "Senators Compromise on Aid for Israel," *New York Times*, March 14, 1992, p. 3.

8   Jackson Diehl and John Goshko, "Israelis Pessimistic On Loan Backing," *Washington Post*, February 24, 1992, pp. A1 and A13.

9   Amy Docsker Marcus, "Some Israelis Say Loan Guarantees May Be Harmful to the Economy," *Wall Street Journal*, February 13, 1992, p. A11.

10   Hirsh Goodman, "No more handouts," *Jerusalem Report*, December 5, 1991, p. 41, and Amy Dockser Marcus, "Public Debate Emerges as Israel Seeks To Reduce Its Dependence on U.S. Aid," *Wall Street Journal*, December 12, 1992.

11   As cited in *Near East Report*, July 27, 1998, p. 70.

12   Clyde Mark, "Israel: Proposed Changes in U.S. Foreign Assistance, FY1999," *CRS Report for Congress*, February 11, 1998; Philip Shenon, "Israel Sketches Out an Overall Drop in U.S. Aid Over Ten Years," *New York Times*, January 29, 1998, p. A5; and Serge Schmemann, "Israelis to Discuss Phasing Out $1.2 Billion U.S. Economic Aid," *New York Times*, January 27, 1998, p. A23.

13   Carla Anne Robbins, "Israeli Aid Could Face A Cutback," *Wall Street Journal*, June 26, 1998, p. 16.

14   Steve Rodan, "Ne'eman Visits U.S. to Finalize Aid Plan," *Jerusalem Post* (internet edition), May 4, 1998.

15   David Makovsky, Nitzan Horowitz, and Sharon Sadeh, "High Hopes for Success at Summit," *Ha'aretz* (English internet edition), October 15, 1998; and David Horowitz, "Israel to Get More U.S. Aid," *Ha'aretz* (English internet edition), October 25, 1998. In an October 25, 1998, interview on CNN Late Edition with Wolf Blitzer, Netanyahu implied the amount requested was more than $1 billion.

16   *Foreign Operations, Export Financing, and Related Programs Appropriations Bill, 1999*, House of Representatives Report 105–719, September 15, 1998, p. 28.

17   *Foreign Operations, Export Financing, and Related Programs Appropriations Bill, 1999*, Senate Report 105–255, July 21, 1998, p. 26.

Chapter 4

Regionwide Cooperation

The United States has been active in a number of initiatives designed to foster peace by involving Israel and its Arab partners in mutually beneficial endeavors. These efforts, including the multilateral track, the Middle East and North Africa (MENA) summits, and the Bank for Economic Cooperation and Development in the Middle East and North Africa (MENABANK), were intended to widen the circle of peace beyond the core parties, to demonstrate the material benefits of peace and cooperation, and to form people-to-people ties across borders. They have met with varying levels of success, but none have managed to escape the damaging spillover effect from political complications in the bilateral negotiations.

THE MULTILATERAL TRACK

The peace process started by U.S. president George Bush's administration in 1991 involved not only direct negotiations between Israel and each Arab party (the bilateral track) but also talks among all the regional states and concerned powers (the multilateral track). Whereas the bilateral negotiations were to focus directly on land disputes, the multilaterals were to address broader regional issues. Members of the Bush administration described the multilateral track as "an essential complement to the bilaterals."[1] President Bush himself said in Madrid in October 1991, when the bilaterals met for the first time, that any peace that does not go beyond nonbelligerency to include economic relations, trade, investment, and even mutual tourism—that is, issues addressed in the multilateral track—will not be a lasting peace.[2] The idea behind the multilateral talks was for the parties to address those regional issues apart from bilateral disputes over land and security.

The logic of holding multilateral talks simultaneously with the bilateral negotiations was that problems such as water usage, the environment, and arms control go beyond specific states or pairs of states, and they are too important to be held hostage to the resolution of land disputes. As an added benefit—and, for the United States, an even higher priority—the process of working together on these issues would create relationships and means of interaction that could carry over into other issues. Sensitive to the potential accusation from the Arab side that the multilateral talks were intended as a substitute for the bilateral negotiations, President Bush said, "To the contrary, progress in the multilateral issues can help create an atmosphere in which long-standing bilateral disputes can more easily be settled."[3]

Some Americans hoped the multilateral track might lure the reluctant Israeli government of Yitzhak Shamir into the Madrid process, but there is little evidence that Shamir himself was particularly eager to normalize relations with Israel's Arab neighbors. Another hope was that the multilateral talks might encourage a sense of momentum and cooperation that would make the bilateral negotiations a little easier and foster improved relations among regional parties. An additional benefit expected from the multilaterals was that the structure of this track gave members of the international community—beyond the U.S. and Russian sponsors—a direct role, and therefore a stake, in the peace process. Participation of Arab states other than those who would be part of the bilateral talks was a way to encourage wider Arab backing for the peace process. In the case of the European Community (EC, now European Union), American officials may have hoped that providing the Europeans with a prominent position in the multilateral talks would keep them busy to prevent them from seeking a central role in the bilateral negotiations.

Despite these potential benefits from the multilateral track, the sponsors generally treated it as a low priority. The opening session of the multilateral talks, held in Moscow at the end of January 1992 (several months after the Madrid conference), stood in stark contrast to both the well-planned and carefully prepared Madrid conference and the subsequent bilateral negotiations in Washington.[4] No clear guidelines, institutional arrangements, or procedural rules were established in advance. Had the sponsors, particularly the United States, taken a somewhat different approach, it might have inoculated the multilateral track to some degree against the ups and downs of the bilateral negotiations.

Even when the talks began, few high-level U.S. government officials devoted much attention or resources to the multilaterals. This may have been because of the paradox of shared international responsibility. U.S. officials had deliberately devised a framework to share the responsibility for the multilaterals with Europe, Canada, Russia, and Japan, as well as with regional parties. As explained bluntly by Edward Djerejian, U.S. assistant secretary of state for Near Eastern and South Asian affairs, the officials invited a wide variety of international parties because they "understood that the U.S. could not afford to shoulder the entire promise and obligation of peace as it had done at Camp David."[5] U.S. officials interviewed also said they had hoped that having many additional parties fully involved would foster the benefits described above. Yet, the division of labor among a number of countries meant that the multilaterals were a secondary concern to many but not the top priority of any powerful country. It also led to the phenomenon of disputes arising among the outside countries, particularly with regard to financial matters, even before tensions among regional parties became a debilitating factor.

The structure of the multilateral talks developed at that opening session included a steering group consisting of the United States, Russia, Israel, Egypt, Jordan and the Palestinians, Saudi Arabia, Tunisia, the EC, Japan, Canada, and, joining later, Norway. The structure also included five working groups to address each of the key regional issues: water resources, the environment, refugees, arms control and regional security, and regional economic development—this last issue in particular being the one discussed here. Djerejian explained that several of the working groups were deliberately designed to address matters that were also key to the bilateral track, in the hope that they would help lay the groundwork for bilateral progress.[6] Unfortunately, the interrelationship between the two tracks also made the progress achieved by technocrats on the various multilateral issues vulnerable to problems that arose in the bilateral track.

In fact, the politics of bilateral conflicts infused the multilateral track even before it began. Syria refused to take part in the Madrid conference unless the sponsors agreed to make participation in the multilateral track voluntary, because Syria and Lebanon refused to attend the multilaterals until bilateral land disputes were resolved.[7] Similarly, the Palestinians boycotted the opening multilateral track meeting because of dissatisfaction over the Madrid terms, which limited their delegation to those living in the West Bank or Gaza. U.S. secretary of state James Baker chided them for this decision, arguing that, with their decision to boycott that meeting, they had "once again passed up an important opportunity."[8] The United States thus had to negotiate between the Arab and Israeli positions on the participation of the EC, the United Nations, and the Palestinians.[9]

Nevertheless, the multilateral track both illustrated and fostered the importance of joint approaches to some of the practical problems facing the region. Syria, although officially boycotting the groups, received individual briefings from the Japanese sponsors after each meeting of the environment working group, and Damascus showed great interest in the proceedings. Moreover, participants did find, sometimes in spite of themselves, that the collaborative nature of the process, along with the infusion of cash and expertise from the international participants, made certain shared problems seem more manageable.

The Regional Economic Development Working Group

The largest of the five working groups (in terms of breadth of projects as well as number of participants), the Regional Economic Development Working Group (REDWG) was also the group that most directly represented the notion that peace could be fostered by, and also be instrumental to, cooperation-based improvements in economic well-being. REDWG's two primary goals were to foster integrated development for the region as a whole based on cooperative solutions to problems, and to make a concerted effort to develop the Palestinian economy. Israel was pleased to have issues of Palestinian economic development addressed in a multilateral working group as opposed to focusing on them in the bilateral negotiations.[10] The EC was designated "gavel holder" for REDWG, with the United States and Japan serving as co-organizers.

Unfortunately, the respective roles of the EC and the United States in REDWG virtually ensured that any competition between them for Middle East influence would reverberate in the functioning and effectiveness of the group. America's proscribed role in it led U.S. officials to try to remove certain key functions, such as the development of the West Bank and Gaza, from the purview of REDWG. The United States convened a donor conference after the September 1993 signing of the Oslo Declaration of Principles (DOP), for example, rather than following the European preference to have all aid administered under the exclusive control of the World Bank.[11] The Europeans objected so strenuously to the prominent U.S. role in coordinating aid that a compromise solution had to be found through an ad hoc committee that reported both to REDWG and to the Multilateral Track Steering Committee.[12] The United States also largely took control of the MENA summits, even though the summits might logically have been a function of REDWG.

The DOP gave both regional and international participants a greater sense of potential, but it also marked the beginning of a decline in the centrality of REDWG. At the fourth round of talks, which was held shortly after the DOP signing, REDWG adopted the Copenhagen Action Plan, which sought to undertake thirty-five varied projects that until then had been discussed only theoretically. One of REDWG's reasons for doing this was to avoid seeing its activities become marginalized.

The steering group of the multilateral track also decided after the Casablanca summit in 1994 to establish a REDWG monitoring committee secretariat as a permanent institution based in Amman. The secretariat was to deal with all sectors under REDWG's purview and to promote regional economic cooperation generally. The secretariat still maintains an office in Amman, but it ceased to play a notable role as REDWG itself became marginalized.

At the urging of the European Union (EU), the regional parties agreed at a meeting in Rabat in June 1994 to establish a small monitoring committee to be staffed primarily by Israelis, Palestinians, Jordanians and Egyptians.[13] The purpose was to give the regional parties a more direct role in REDWG and, particularly, in implementing the Copenhagen Action Plan. Disagreements over the exact composition of the committee delayed the preliminary meeting until December 1994, at which time it was decided to have two chairs—one for the EU and one a rotating chair held by one of the core regional parties.[14] The substantive work of the REDWG monitoring committee was divided among four sectoral committees—finance, infrastructure, trade, and tourism—whose membership consisted solely of representatives from the four core parties. The broad scope and wide variety of initiatives falling under the auspices of the infrastructure committee led to the establishment of several steering groups dealing with such particular aspects as transport and the integration of the region's electricity grids.

The tourism committee had one of REDWG's more publicized successes, with the establishment of the Middle East and Mediterranean Travel and Tourism Association (MEMTTA), whose charter was signed during the MENA summit in Amman in October 1995. MEMTTA's aim was to encourage tourism to the region, to develop public and private sector cooperation on tourism issues, and to facilitate the movement of tourists among different regional states. Even with the peace process going fairly well, the establishment of MEMTTA was not seamless. It suffered a series of delays and setbacks before the charter was completed and approved. Until the political process reached an impasse, however, MEMTTA seemed like a particularly promising initiative. Tourism is one area in which none of the core parties is achieving its full potential—all have excellent draws, simply in terms of history and other attractions—and an improvement for one could easily serve as a boost to all the others.

Even before the 1996 change in the Israeli government and the increased political difficulties facing the peace process, REDWG encountered serious difficulties. Whereas its goals were far-reaching and its initiatives expensive, it had no funding mechanism. It suffered from the U.S.–European rivalry, and commercial competitiveness colored the feasibility studies that various donor countries conducted. Regional leaders generally do not portray those donor rivalries as a source of problems in the multilaterals or in the peace process as a whole, but these tensions undoubtedly decreased the effectiveness of REDWG. The United States angered the Europeans by acknowledging their investments of money and other resources but at the same time denying them the influence they thought they deserved. This tension has been a constant backdrop to international economic efforts related to the peace process.[15]

Prospects for the Multilateral Track
Progress on the multilateral track has been closely linked to progress on the bilateral track. For instance, after the DOP, most of the REDWG committees started holding their meetings in the region for the first time, signifying the increased openness among Arab parties that stemmed from bilateral progress. Then—ironically—just at the moment when the improvement in the Israeli–Palestinian bilateral track was invigorating REDWG, the subsequent deterioration in both the political negotiations and the Palestinian economic situation boded ill for REDWG. Many Arab states refused to attend the 1997 MENA summit at Doha because of the stalemate in the Israeli–Palestinian bilateral track, and most Arab countries pulled back from the multilaterals on those grounds as well. For example, nearly all Arab countries refused to attend a meeting of the multilateral steering committee and working groups scheduled in Moscow for March 1997. Israel blamed Egypt for delaying its decision on whether to attend, because other Arab states were conditioning their attendance on Egypt's. Israel also blamed the United States for failing to pressure Egypt to sanction the event. IDF Radio quoted a "high-ranking Jerusalem source" saying that this was "another step in the transformation of the normalization of Israel's relations with Arab countries into a hostage of the negotiations with the Palestinians."[16] With many Arab governments and their citizens having long thought of the multilaterals primarily as a reward for Israel, the arguments of states like Syria—that normalization should await full Israeli withdrawal from disputed territory—gained widespread currency.

According to this line of thinking, premature normalization rewards Israel for obstinacy and relinquishes a potential tool for pressing Israel on bilateral issues.[17]

Once the bilateral Israeli–Palestinian negotiations entered the eighteen-month stalemate—which ended only with the Wye summit in October 1998—even sponsors like the United States appeared to lose interest in the multilateral track. To the extent that international parties were involved in the peace process during those eighteen months, the focus was on bilateral political issues.

The Wye River Memorandum has not enjoyed the enthusiasm the Oslo DOP did, largely because of increased cynicism on all sides that an agreement made will not necessarily be implemented. Yet, during the weeks following the Wye signing, the U.S. government indicated that it expected this reinvigoration of the bilateral peace process to result in a resumption of the multilateral track and the trend toward normalization between Israel and the Arabs.[18] This will be a challenge; most Arab parties appear to prefer maintaining a wait-and-see approach rather than resuming multilateral activity before the terms of the Wye Memorandum are fulfilled and final status talks between the Israelis and Palestinians show signs of progress.

In the effort to reinvigorate the multilateral track, certain lessons from the past seven years may offer useful guideposts. First, with regard to REDWG in particular, a greater degree of coordination between the United States and the EU would help. At the very least there should be enough coordination to avoid situations of overlapping and competing institutions, as well as conflicting positions on basic issues. Two months after Wye, the United States and the EU issued a joint declaration on the peace process, citing a commitment on both their parts to work for, among other things, the "early resumption of the Multilateral Track of the Process."[19] If the coordination exhibited in this joint declaration is carried over into the practical work on the multilaterals, these talks will have a better chance for success.

Second, although no issue in the Middle East is free from political overtones and underpinnings, it is often productive to address problems on the most technical level possible. Meetings conducted by technical experts have a better record at withstanding political ups and downs than do large plenary meetings. The latter, in fact, almost entirely ceased after the stalemate in the Israeli–Palestinian track became apparent in 1996, whereas expert-level meetings continued in several working groups, such as the environment and the water groups.

Part of the eagerness of U.S. officials to restart the multilateral process in the wake of Wye stems from the desire to have visible signs that peace is progressing. Yet, one of the reasons expert-level meetings have been more resilient than large political gatherings is the lack of publicity that meetings of technical experts generate. Thus, a third lesson is that the avoidance of publicity has given participants in such meetings freedom from the hindrance of constant scrutiny and criticism, especially on the part of skeptics.

A fourth lesson is that meetings consisting of participants from coordinating outside parties and only those countries directly affected by a particular issue are often more successful than those which include all of the regional parties. This has especially proven true when an issue involves only Israel and Jordan, or only those two and the Palestinians, when the Egyptians do not need to be involved. For example, long after the working group on the environment stopped holding plenary meetings, Japan and the United States cosponsored a meeting of Israel, the Palestinian Authority (PA), and Jordan on regional environmental issues. They addressed practical solutions to shared problems like the overabundance of flies and mosquitoes.[20]

MENA SUMMITS

Four MENA summits have taken place since they were started as part of the peace process. The first was held in Casablanca in 1994, the second in Amman in 1995, the third in Cairo in 1996, and the latest (and perhaps final) conference was in Doha in 1997. The conferences evolved along with the peace process, with the focus and participant list each year reflecting political developments. Behind-the-scenes contacts between Israelis and Arabs at the conferences also changed with the status of the peace process.

The summits were conceived as an effort to highlight and encourage the multilateral aspects of the peace process. Sponsored by the United States and Russia and organized by the New York-based Council on Foreign Relations and the Davos, Switzerland–based World Economic Forum, the MENA summits brought regional parties together and invited outside businesspeople to find investment opportunities in a newly stable region. By doing so, the summits were supposed to infuse private money into the region and show the profitability of normalization. Each regional state was allowed not only a delegation of businesspeople, but also a forum in which to highlight its own reforms, growth, and investment opportunities. Potential investors valued the opportunity to have direct contact with high-level government officials from regional states in which they were considering doing business. Sponsors were also pleased at the prospect of people-to-people ties that could develop among Arab and Israeli businesspeople at the summits.

Casablanca

The Casablanca summit took place during the halcyon days of the peace process. Jordan and Israel had just signed their peace treaty, the Israel–Palestinian Declaration of Principles was new and seemed promising, Israel and Syria were engaged in serious talks, and several Arab states were taking steps away from the boycott and toward ties with Israel. With the notable exception of Syria and Lebanon, who stayed away in protest the event, and Iraq and Libya, who were not invited, all Arab states took part in the Casablanca summit. It was one of the first concrete manifestations of the peace process and its promise of lucrative normalization.

The delegation of each participating state was led by high-level political officials, including kings, princes, prime ministers, and foreign ministers. About 2,000 businesspeople also attended as delegates from their respective countries, including representatives of almost 150 U.S. companies. Israel was represented disproportionately, with nine ministers and other members of Knesset attending in addition to a large contingent from the private sector. Unfortunately, the large and enthusiastic Israeli delegation reinforced the impression among some Arab critics that the primary purpose of the summit was actually to benefit Israel's political and economic positions in the region.

At the time of the summit, the potential for cooperation seemed limitless. The language in the Casablanca Declaration is indicative of the great hope participants had for peace and particularly for the role economics could play in achieving and sustaining peace. The declaration refers to the commitment of governments present to show that "business can do business and contribute to peace as well; indeed, to prove that profitability contributes mightily to the economic scaffolding for a durable peace."[21]

The U.S. government pushed Middle East leaders and the U.S. business community to attend the Casablanca summit and make it succeed. U.S. officials did not expect major deals to be concluded there, especially with corporations newly exposed to the region, but they were determined to ensure that the summit did have meaningful results. Thus, they announced the establishment of a number of regional projects and institutions, including the MEMTTA regional tourist board and a steering committee to address all multilateral issues. Assessing each of these institutions five years later is sobering, but at the time of the Casablanca summit hopes were high that the peace process and the economic institutions being formed to foster it would proceed apace and thrive. Participants pledged in the final declaration "to transform this event into lasting institutional and individual ties that will provide a better life for the peoples" of the region.[22]

In the perspective of the deteriorating situation of the late 1990s, it is easy to idealize the memory of the Casablanca summit as a time when the Middle East was awash in peaceful sentiments. Interviews for this project almost uniformly elicited descriptions of a summit that epitomized hope for a future of cooperation and prosperity for all. In fact, some participants complain in retrospect that the summit in Morocco was dominated by political euphoria, with business taking a back seat to symbolism and dramatic speeches. Although this is true in a relative sense—that is, when compared to the prevailing attitudes at subsequent summits—analysis of the speeches and media coverage at the time of the Casablanca summit indicate that opposition in the Arab world was widespread even then.

Casablanca's critics can be divided into two general categories: those who were concerned that the normalization was outpacing the bilateral negotiations, and those who feared that Israel was using economics as a means to secure its acceptance in the region without making any political concessions.[23] Neither type of critic participated in the summit, however, and the regional businesspeople who did attend not only displayed a sense of optimism that the peace process would continue, but were eager both to encourage it and to benefit from it.

Political leaders attending Casablanca also illustrated this sense of optimism. Morocco's King Hassan and Israel's then–foreign minister, Shimon Peres, made speeches filled with hopeful language and peaceful imagery. The speech by U.S. secretary of state Warren Christopher described a situation in which a peace between governments had been achieved (or was at least well within reach) and now needed to be cemented by economic growth and cooperation with private sector involvement. The concerns Christopher expressed were not about enemies of peace but rather about economic policies that had combined with political instability to prevent the countries of the region from being as attractive to outside investors as they otherwise might have been.

Later summits made the opportunity to focus on positive political trends, or even on economic needs and plans, seem like a lost and much-missed luxury. An Israeli background paper on the Casablanca summit, issued by the Government Press Office, captured Casablanca's strong sense of optimism. The paper stated that the summit "marks a new stage of the peace process—the transition from peace-making to peace-strengthening." Four years later that sentiment appears to have been, at best, premature.

Amman

The Amman Summit, held in October 1995, was slightly less of a political show than was Casablanca, although the level of political representation was still high, with the U.S. delegation again headed by Secretary of State Christopher. As an additional sign of the value the administration placed on the MENA process and regional economic cooperation, Commerce Secretary Ron Brown joined him. The Israeli delegation was also large and impressive, but—in a conscious attempt to reduce the impression that the summit was first and foremost an Israeli integration festival—it was somewhat smaller than that which attended the Casablanca summit.

Even though the Amman summit took place before the assassination of Israeli prime minister Yitzhak Rabin and the later election of Binyamin Netanyahu as prime minister, it was becoming clear that the MENA summits' political character would make them vulnerable to the ups and downs of the peace process. Whereas the speeches at the Casablanca summit had contained some references to hostilities, several statements at the Amman meeting were openly doubtful of the peace process and expressed concern about normalization outpacing land-for-peace solutions to political conflicts. Most notable was the speech by Egyptian foreign minister Amre Moussa, which was not only highly critical of Israel and insistent upon a comprehensive peace preceding full normalization, but also took Jordan to task in a thinly veiled admonishment for its rush to full peace with Israel.[24]

The Amman Declaration was positive in terms of its assessments of the peace process and ambitious plans for economic institutions. Many of the pledges, however, illustrated that little progress had been made since the ideas were initially raised at the Casablanca summit. The regional bank and business council first discussed the year before were still on the agenda, but they were also still described in the future tense.

One sign of the prestige enjoyed by the MENA summit process and the peace process itself at the time of the Amman summit was the eagerness of regional states to host future summits. Both Egypt and Qatar volunteered to host the next summit, ultimately deciding that the next one would be in Cairo and the one after that in Doha. Much was to change before the next meeting, however, challenging the status of the MENA summits and shaking the optimism about the peace process that had made economic openness seem so feasible.

Cairo

By the time the Cairo summit was to take place, the Israeli government had changed hands and the peace process had entered a period of difficulty. The Egyptian government hesitated to go ahead with the summit and faced great pressure within the Arab world to cancel it. Syria in particular went beyond boycotting the event and put a great deal of pressure on Egypt not to host it at all. At the strong urging of the Americans, the event did take place, but at Egypt's request the summit was downgraded to a conference, with the level of political representation leading the delegations appropriately lowered. Egyptian officials also made a point of focusing on the potential benefits for Egypt and the possibilities for deals among Arab states. Some Egyptian economists and businesspeople interviewed said that the summits, and particularly the Cairo conference, played the useful role of forcing their government to address economic issues from a larger, even global, perspective. As justification for going ahead with the event, the Egyptians implied that they thought the conference should be used by Arab attendees to network with each other and with outside investors; Israelis were to be treated as an unavoidable nuisance.

Not only was the level of political representation diminished; the tone of the speeches was also a far cry from what had been heard at Casablanca and Amman, hints of trouble at those first two summits notwithstanding. The closing line of Egyptian president Husni Mubarak's speech opening the conference summed up the odd combination of hope, fear, and urgency that characterized the thinking of many leaders at the time of the Cairo conference: "We are reaching today for our future. Together let us not lose sight of it. Together let us build it, build a peace that is just, build a prosperity that is for all. For it shall not be said, centuries from today, that our countries had peace within their grasp and squandered it."[25] Meanwhile, political leaders at the Cairo conference concentrated on the peace process deadlock du jour—an agreement on the Hebron redeployment—rather than on economics.

Cairo was the largest of the MENA conferences, with more than 4,000 participants, but few Palestinian businesspeople attended, because of anger and frustration over Israeli policies. Participants registered concern over the worsening economic conditions facing the Palestinians and the affect this would ultimately have on the potential for peace and prosperity in the region. The Cairo Declaration states that "removing restrictive measures and closures will prevent the decline of, and contribute positively to the performance of the Palestinian economy, as well as the political atmosphere surrounding the peace process in its entirety."[26]

For the sponsors and for participants who were primarily concerned with the MENA summits as a booster to the peace process, the worsening tone and reduced political participation were troubling. From the perspective of some of the business participants, however, the diminished role of political symbolism was a positive side effect of the worsening state of the peace process. Business was able to proceed and to enjoy a more prominent status. Whereas the presence of political officials is desirable to businesspeople, the ideal would be for the officials to be accessible rather than dominant. Potential investors wanted to see the politicians as facilitators rather than as the reason for the event. In that regard, each MENA summit (or conference) was an improvement over the one preceding it.

Doha

The fourth MENA conference, held in Doha in November 1997, was more memorable for the controversy leading up to it than for anything that happened at the conference itself. Similarly, it was more notable for the regional countries that shunned it than for those that attended. Qatar had to resist tremendous pressure from the Arab world to cancel. Like Egypt did for the Cairo conference, Qatar asked the sponsors to downgrade the meeting from a summit to a conference, but U.S. allies like Egypt and Saudi Arabia completely boycotted the conference anyway.

The role of the United States as the prime supporter and defender of the MENA summit process was apparent and became a subject of controversy on its own merits. For months before the Doha conference, it was clear that there would be a problem with regional attendance. The peace process was in a difficult period, and there was some tension between the U.S. administration and the Israeli government. Just before the conference began, Israel Television reported that senior U.S. officials were blaming Israeli prime minister Binyamin Netanyahu for the collapse of efforts to bring Arab countries to the Doha conference.[27] Nevertheless, high-level U.S. officials energetically advocated the conference, flying around the region urging allies and friends to attend, and arguing (quite irrefutably) that the Middle East was sorely in need of outside investment and regional integration. They cited the low level of interregional trade and the fact that, even excluding Israel, inter-Arab trade was only 7 percent. They also maintained that the MENA conferences were not a favor to Israel, but a benefit to all parties in the region.[28] One former U.S. ambassador even made the explicit argument that the Cairo conference had "already established the precedent that the annual economic summit has now become a primarily economic [and] commercial gathering rather than a political one."[29]

The Middle East has less interregional trade than does any other region of the world. The Arabs who resisted the conference, however, were more concerned with the political symbolism than with possible economic gains. They were also unconvinced that attendance at the MENA conferences brought significant benefits to any country other than the host and, of course, Israel. Moreover, there was some suspicion about what was making the United States push so enthusiastically for attendance at this summit. One Egyptian daily urged the boycotting countries to adhere to their stance even more firmly in response to the misguided American push to attend.[30]

The few Arab countries that attended, like Jordan, sent lower-level officials. To the chagrin of the United States, even the Israeli foreign minister, David Levy, made a last-minute decision to stay away from Doha. Two of the three hosts of the previous MENA conferences, Egypt and Morocco, boycotted this conference altogether, although businesspeople from those and other boycotting states attended as part of other countries' delegations. Yet, many businesspeople and professional associations chose to boycott the conference even if their governments were sending delegations.

To the extent that politics permeated the event itself (and not just the build-up to it), participants and speeches accurately reflected the prevailing level of impatience and anger both with the stalls in the peace process and, more specifically, with the Netanyahu government. The closing declaration urged Israel to abide by the land-for-peace principles in the peace process and in UN Security Council Resolutions 242 and 338. The Israeli delegation, led by Industry and Trade Minister Natan Sharansky, tried unsuccessfully to block the declaration, taking issue with the reference to land-for-peace. Despite, or perhaps because of, their role in pushing for the conference, U.S. officials fully participated in the expressions of anger and impatience with Netanyahu during the summit. The *Financial Times* described the conference as "three days' constant criticism of Israel, with the U.S. often leading the way. . ."[31]

As with the Cairo conference, however, the politically troubled background did not detract from, and actually may have enhanced, the positive business atmosphere at the conference. The Doha conference took place at a smaller venue than did the Cairo conference, with much of the conference and guest facilities built specifically for the event; therefore, despite a smaller number of attendees, the conference was attended to capacity. In the end, even Israeli industrialists and officials said that they were pleased with how the conference turned out, despite the anger and criticism targeted at Israel. Israeli businesspeople claimed to have had extensive contacts with Arab counterparts—even more so than at previous conferences—although many of these contacts were conducted in secrecy.

Leading Israeli businessman Benny Ga'on summed up the view of many of the businesspeople present when he said, "I didn't miss the politicians. I didn't come to visit them."[32]

Policy Issues

The affect of the MENA summits and conferences on the peace process is difficult to gauge, as the goals of the summits are more long-term (or at least medium-term) than they are immediate. The meetings certainly did not result in enough deals for enough people to alter quickly the economies of any of the countries; it would have been unrealistic to assume or even hope that they would. The more modest goals of promoting people-to-people ties among regional businesspeople, and of drawing the attention of potential outside investors to the region, may have had some success. Regional businesspeople interviewed for this project favorably assessed these particular results of the meetings. Unfortunately, the process of showing potential outside investors that the Middle East had changed and was "open for business" was interrupted by a reversion to an atmosphere characterized by instability.

In April 1998, the World Economic Forum officially suspended the annual conferences. It was adamant that it was not canceling them, and that it will be ready to proceed with vigor as soon as political conditions permit. Meetings early in 1998 had failed to determine a venue for the next MENA summit, primarily because no country volunteered to host it. The consensus is that the future of the MENA summits depends on the direction of the peace process. Whereas none of the parties involved suggested an official declaration that the MENA summit process be declared dead, most supported a decision to hold off on planning another summit until the peace process shows some political progress. They insisted that the next one come when movement in the peace process provides the potential for a meaningful gathering, not simply when twelve months have passed on the calendar.

The breakthrough achieved at Wye in October 1998 left the U.S. administration with a decision as to whether or not to attempt a MENA summit in 1999. There had been some talk at the Doha meeting about holding a future summit in Bethlehem, and this possibility has been revisited in the months following the Wye summit. The lessons of the post-Oslo years indicate, however, that rushing into a large-scale effort to push a reluctant region into a summit would be ill-advised. Yet, although the idea of a grand summit is impractical absent substantial political change, the United States or the World Economic Forum could encourage or sponsor events on a smaller scale, possibly with a different focus. U.S. leaders can consider making an attempt to get the regional players together to encourage economic cooperation and foreign investment in the economies of the peace process participants in a less politicized format.

A number of regional players and attendees of prior conferences have made the point that the primary benefits are in the area of people-to-people contacts and drawing the attention of international business people to the region. From the point of view of U.S. diplomatic interests, the primary benefits from the conferences come when they give a symbolic boost to the state of regional relations and when they foster a constituency for peace among the region's businesspeople. The conferences achieve the latter goal by promoting the belief that an image of cooperation attracts outside investors. The question U.S. policymakers must ask themselves, then, is what type of conference, if any, will be worth their efforts in terms of having these results.

By definition, the type of conferences prescribed by some in the region—small specialized meetings of businesspeople with no direct political component—might be quite useful, but they would not be appropriate arenas for the active involvement of the U.S. government. If such conferences were to be organized, the commerce and state departments could certainly make themselves available as advisers or consultants to the private-sector organizers. They could also encourage private companies based in the United States to attend and to pursue projects. In such a scenario, the U.S. government would have neither the glory nor the risk that was associated with the four summits, and the trade-off may therefore be worthwhile.

Meetings organized in this way would potentially serve the purpose of promoting people-to-people ties among business elites, and thus of encouraging a constituency for peace. The drawback from a U.S. standpoint is that these meetings would not provide widespread publicity for a new, cooperative image of the region. On the other hand, as illustrated by the Doha conference, the publicity of a large, official conference can backfire when the desired image is clearly contradicted by the reality in the region.

MENABANK

Proposals for a multilateral Middle East development bank, along the lines of the Asian Development Bank or the Inter-American Development Bank, have a long history. The idea gained support during the administration of U.S. president Jimmy Carter, and the Center for Strategic and International Studies in 1982 organized two international conferences to flesh out a proposal for a Middle East development fund.[33] In his major policy address during the Gulf War, then–Secretary of State James Baker committed the United States to the creation of such an institution.[34]

Each time, the idea foundered primarily for political reasons: Most Arab states—especially the rich Gulf states that were expected to be primary financial contributors—would not join a bank to which Israel belonged, but the United States would not join unless Israel was fully integrated into the bank's operations, and the Europeans were not interested unless the United States and most Arab countries were involved. There was skepticism about the bank on both economic and political grounds. Most countries in the area already had high debt loads, so more debt was not necessarily appropriate. And existing multilateral banks— the World Bank, the African Development Bank (to which Egypt, Morocco, Tunisia, and Algeria are vitally important, as they are the ADB's most creditworthy borrowers), and the Arab Development Fund—were vigorously active in the Arab countries, evaluating projects and making loans. As for Israel, it enjoyed excellent access to international finance and did not need to put up with all the paperwork involved in working a multilateral development bank, which would evaluate projects closely rather than rely on the say-so of the local authorities. The Middle East bank idea, never very active, became even less attractive to the industrial countries when they viewed the teething problems of the European Bank for Reconstruction and Development (EBRD), set up after the fall of the Berlin Wall to help Eastern Bloc countries. Despite a charter designed to reduce bureaucratic barriers, the EBRD in its first two years of operation spent more on its own administrative expenses than it disbursed in loans.

In 1993, in a statement that reflects his attitude toward the private sector, then–Foreign Minister Shimon Peres wrote, "I believe . . . it is preferable to concentrate all investment money for Middle Eastern development in a bank set up exclusively for that purpose."[35] At least in part because of his urging, and despite considerable opposition within the U.S. government up to the last minute, President Bill Clinton, when speaking to the Jordanian parliament in October 1994, said, "The United States supports the creation of a Middle East Bank for Cooperation and Development. And we will take the lead in consultations with governments within and beyond the region to ensure that the bank is properly structured."[36] The next week, at the Casablanca economic summit, the United States submitted a proposal for a bank.[37]

The idea generated more opposition than support.[38] Many Europeans and Gulf Arabs saw the bank as something they would be expected to

finance but concerning which they would have little input. Europeans preferred to provide their assistance through existing institutions, and the Gulf
states thought the bank would benefit Israel.[39] Europeans suspected that
the United States was making an end-run around the European-dominated
REDWG. On top of that, the Europeans had been going through the difficulties with the EBRD, and they saw the MENABANK proposal as re-
peating the worst aspects of that experience—a heavy bureaucratic structure
competing to lend to a region already afloat with offers to finance projects.
The EU proposed that instead of a development bank, an institution be
created to assess the feasibility of specific projects and to secure funding
for them from elsewhere.[40] A task force on alternative funding mechanisms
for the region met in January, March, April, May, and July 1995. In interviews, senior officials from various countries portrayed the U.S. attitude
as dismissive of the European and Gulf criticisms. U.S. officials, according to those interviewed, seemed to view the criticisms as surmountable,
given enough pressure, and in any case politically motivated rather than
genuinely economic. According to those interviewed, Americans believed
that the MENABANK critics disliked a U.S. leadership role and betrayed
a lack of commitment to promoting cooperation between Arabs and Israel.
Indeed, those were certainly elements in the European response; the aid
programs undertaken by the EU and its member states have been singu-
larly uninterested in cooperation between Israel and Arabs, focusing exclusively on the national development of individual Arab states and on
cooperation among Arab countries.

Contrary to U.S. expectations, the prospects for the bank were only
mixed—despite continuing U.S. pressure—until mid-1995. It was only
then that the four core peace process partners—Israel, the PA, Jordan, and
Egypt—swung solidly behind the MENABANK concept. The support came
initially from the foreign ministries among the partners, with finance ministries not necessarily supportive until later. Indeed, although initially quite
opposed to the proposal for a bank, the Israeli finance ministry eventually
supported it because the bank proposal was the first thing that the four
core partners had devised on their own and therefore it behooved everyone
to bend over backwards for it, even if it was only a marginally good thing.
As Secretary of State Christopher said in his opening remarks at the Amman
summit, "The bank's establishment is a major milestone—not least because it is the first initiative put forward by the parties to the peace process
themselves."[41] The Israeli decision to support the proposal was strongly
influenced by the fact that Jordan supported an idea for which Egypt was
pushing hard, for the Israelis know that Jordan was generally suspicious of

Egyptian initiatives. In addition, the timing of the proposal fit with the desire, both by the United States and the core partners, to have something major to announce at the October 1995 summit.

In the hours before the summit opened, the United States and the four core peace process partners secured an agreement that, at the very end of the conference they would announce the founding of the bank, with the details to be negotiated by the end of 1995.[42] But after the summit, the United States was unable to overcome the opposition of the Gulf Arab countries or most EU states. Thus it was not until February 1996 that an agreement on MENABANK's charter was reached by four EU states—Italy, the Netherlands, Greece, and Austria—joined with eight other extraregional members (Canada, Cyprus, Japan, Korea, Malta, Turkey and the United States) and seven regional members (Algeria, Egypt, Israel, Jordan, Morocco, the Palestinian Authority, and Tunisia). In the allocation of shares, a large bloc (24.5 percent of the initial $5 billion capitalization) was left unsubscribed in the expectation that several additional industrial countries would join once the bank was up and running. The charter drew on the best practices of other multilateral development banks: It allowed lending to the private sector without the guarantee of the borrowing government, and it mandated that the bank's executive board not be a permanent bureaucracy. Yet, the charter had a significant weakness: It presented the bank as another development institution, not as a peace-promotion institution. No provision was made for putting priority on cooperative projects, as distinct from projects entirely within one country. The bank's charter included a chapter on economic cooperation, but that chapter referred only to the creation of a forum for "dissension and dialogue," which "shall have no authority over other organs of the bank"—and that forum's tasks were framed in purely economic terms (such as, "a conducive environment for entrepreneurial activity") without explicit mention of promoting peace and understanding among peoples.[43]

Once the participants agreed on the bank charter, the Clinton administration turned to getting congressional approval for membership and appropriation for the initial $25 million that the United States was to contribute in cash (only one-fourth of each country's capital contribution had to be in cash; the rest was a guarantee to provide funds if needed to repay money the bank would borrow on international capital markets). Congress had many misgivings about the bank, however. Part of the problem was a general skepticism in the funding committees toward multilateral development banks, as well as skepticism about the specific MENABANK plans—the committees being unsympathetic to a bank that finances public infrastructure projects and unconvinced that a government-financed institution, rather than private capital markets, would be the best source of finance for private business ventures. Added to that was a prohibition against adding to the overall amount of aid going to the Middle East, which would necessitate that funding for the bank be deducted from aid to another project or state in the region. Furthermore, by 1997, the enthusiasm of the core peace process partners for the bank idea had visibly cooled, especially as the peace process developed more and more problems. The Egyptian government, for one, did little if anything to promote the bank, even though its headquarters was to be in Cairo.

But the kiss of death, in addition to congressional skepticism, was the fact that the administration seemed to make MENABANK a low priority. Although the bank's Articles of Agreement were finalized on February 14, 1996, the Clinton administration waited until November 22, 1996—after the Cairo conference—to sign them, much less submit them for Senate consideration. Participants in the various parts of the process whom the authors interviewed for this research all agreed that the administration either did not raise or did not emphasize to Congress the need to appropriate the initial $25 million for MENABANK at critical steps in the congressional cycle. Furthermore, when the proposals were put forward in 1997 to redirect some of the aid money from Israel and Egypt to a fund to support the peace process in general, no one spoke up vigorously for MENABANK, which that year received only interim U.S. financing for its skeleton staff. Those interviewed had the clear impression that the administration preferred to see the redirected aid money go directly to Jordan rather than to MENABANK. In December 1997, and again in March 1998, MENABANK's skeleton staff presented its case to congressional staff, but in the end, the administration made little effort to secure funding, and the issue died. The MENABANK skeleton staff was disbanded in December 1998. The most likely prospect is that MENABANK will wither away without ever becoming active.

Policy Issues

The MENABANK project has to be considered in the light of its political context, not solely on whether it is, in the abstract, a good idea. Because the United States committed its prestige to the creation of the bank, Congress should not have blocked the bank's start-up unless weighty reasons existed.

To be sure, MENABANK is marginal economically. It is hard to argue the region lacks access to capital markets. The bank's role in financing a project would be not so much to provide finance as to provide an implicit guarantee against political problems, on the theory that any project the bank finances would have the implicit endorsement of the relevant government. But that is a function that the World Bank could and would gladly fulfill.

Nor is it clear if MENABANK would have much impact on cementing peace. It is not clear if the bank, once funded, would focus on finding projects that will help to promote peace; the bank's charter and the initial project proposals prepared by the staff seem to be overwhelmingly economic rather than peace-promoting. The economic projects may end up promoting peace only insofar as they make the region more prosperous and thus more oriented toward cooperating whenever there is economic advantage toward doing so; however, that would happen only over the long term.

The failure to design and to market MENABANK as a peace bank was a missed opportunity. MENABANK could be redesigned to promote peace more directly if it were mandated to give priority to projects involving Israel and the Arab peace partners, such as the joint Jordanian–Israeli airport for the Eilat and Aqaba area, or pollution abatement at the head of the Gulf of Aqaba (in the waters of Egypt, Israel, Jordan, and Saudi Arabia), or roads from Egypt to Jordan across Israel and the PA. MENABANK could also be directed to give special priority to projects involving Israel and the PA. For instance, it could be an instrument to bring international expertise to the delicate issue of Palestinian transport between the West Bank and Gaza; passage of trucks across transit countries that do not welcome these trucks and want them tightly controlled is, after all, an area in which the EU has much expertise, including on how to use road improvements to facilitate tighter controls. Whereas few would argue that finances are the central impediment to implementing "safe passage," cost does arise as one element of contention between the Israelis and the Palestinians.

In short, there could be a role for a redesigned MENABANK, especially if it were politically desirable to demonstrate that regional cooperation remains alive.

NOTES

1   Edward P. Djerejian, assistant secretary for Near Eastern affairs, "The Multilateral Talks in the Arab–Israeli Peace Process," address at the Washington Institute for Near East Policy, September 22, 1993, in U.S. Department of State *Dispatch* 4, no. 41 (October 11, 1993), p. 696.

2   George Bush, "Remarks at the Opening Session of the Middle East Peace Conference in Madrid, Spain," October 30, 1991, in *Weekly Compilation of Presidential Documents* 27, no. 44 (November 4, 1991), p. 1543.

3   Ibid., p. 1544.

4   Joel Peters, *Pathways to Peace: The Multilateral Arab–Israeli Peace Talks* (London: Royal Institute of International Affairs, 1996), p. 8.

5   Djerejian, "The Multilateral Talks in the Arab–Israeli Peace Process," p. 697.

6   Ibid.

7   Dalia Dassa Kaye, "Madrid's Forgotten Forum: The Middle East Multilaterals," *Washington Quarterly* 20, no. 1 (Winter 1997), p. 185.

8   James Baker, "Organizational Meeting for Multilateral Negotiations on the Middle East," opening remarks by Secretary Baker in Moscow, January 28, 1992, in U.S. Department of State *Dispatch* 3, supplement no. 2 (February 1992), pp. 27–28.

9   Dassa Kaye, "Madrid's Forgotten Forum," p. 171.

10 "Multilateral Talks," briefing paper on Round Two of the multilateral talks, published and distributed by the Israeli Foreign Ministry, November 24, 1992.

11 World Bank, "Developing the Occupied Territories: An Investment in Peace, Volume II: The Economy" (September 1993). The bank report was discussed as a major REDWG achievement; see Daniel Shapiro, "The Multilateral Talks: Poised for Real Progress?" *Middle East Insight* (September–October 1993), pp. 28–29.

12 Peters, *Pathways to Peace*, p. 48.

13 Ibid., pp. 48–49.

14 Ibid., p. 49.

15 Judy Dempsey, "Santer Backs Palestinians," *Financial Times*, February 9, 1998. See also Francesca Ciriaci, "Jordan, EU Working Closely to Ensure Being 'Associated' with Final Status Talks—Moritanos," *Jordan Times*, December 10, 1998. Joseph Kopel, "European Leaders Complain that U.S. Dominates Mideast," *Jewish Telegraphic Agency*, May 10, 1996.

16 "Egypt, U.S. Seen Responsible for 'Torpedoing' Multilaterals," *IDF Radio*, March 25, 1997, in Foreign Broadcast Information Service, Near East and South Asia, FBIS-NES-97-084, March 25, 1997.

17 The adoption of these views by most other Arab parties was discussed by Nabil Sha'ath, Palestinian Minister of Planning and International Cooperation, in an interview with Lima Nabil in *Al-Ra'y*, "Sha'th on Palestinian State, Peace Talks," August 27, 1998, p. 9, in FBIS-NES-98-239, August 27, 1998. The Syrian argument was explained by Muwaffaq al-'Allaf, then–head of the Syrian delegation to the Madrid peace talks, in "Syria's al-Allaf on Multilaterals," SANA, May 8, 1993, in FBIS-NES-93-088, May 10, 1993, p. 5.

18 Steven Erlanger, "Back Peace, U.S. Urges Arab Allies," *New York Times*, October 27, 1998.

19 "White House U.S.–EU Declaration on the Peace Process," press release issued by the White House, December 18, 1998, available from U.S. Newswire.

by the White House, December 18, 1998, available from U.S. Newswire.

20 "Joint Israel–Jordan–PA Meeting on Environment," Israel Foreign Ministry statement, November 24, 1998.

21 "Casablanca Declaration," *U.S. Department of State Dispatch* 5, no. 45 (November 7, 1994), p. 735

22 Ibid.

23 "No Arab Cheers for Casablanca," *Mideast Mirror*, November 1, 1994.

24 Jack Redden, "Egypt Tells Summit MidEast Economy Tied to Peace," *Reuters*, October 31, 1995. See also "Egyptian–Jordanian 'Tongue-Lashing' Sets Quarrelsome Tone at Opening of Regional Economic Summit," *Mideast Mirror*, October 30, 1995.

25 "Inter-Arab Affairs: Mubarak Addresses Economic Conference," Cairo ESC Television, November 12, 1996, in FBIS-NES-96-219, November 12, 1996.

26 "Cairo Economic Summit Declaration," November 1996, available online at http://www.usia.gov/regional/nea/econmena/cairdecl.htm/.

27 Ehud Ya'ari, "Israel: U.S. Holds Netanyahu 'Responsible' for Arabs Shunning Doha," Israel Television Channel 1 Network, November 12, 1997, in FBIS-NES-97-316, November 12, 1997.

28 This point—that the summits were not a favor to Israel but a benefit to all regional parties—was made, for example, by Martin Indyk during a meeting with Egyptian foreign minister Amre Moussa shortly before the conference; see "U.S. Envoy Urges Egypt to Attend Mideast meeting," *Reuters*, October 30, 1997. James Rubin, in his State Department briefing on November 3, 1997, also made this point: "We don't believe it is a favor to one side or the other."

29 Robert H. Pelletreau, "Why the Doha Summit Should be Held," *Mideast Mirror*, September 29, 1997. An Arabic translation of this article had appeared the previous weekend as an op-ed in the pan-Arab *al-Hayat*.

30 "Egyptian Daily Faults U.S. 'Insistence' on Doha Conference," Middle East News Agency, October 23, 1997, in FBIS-NES-97-296, October 23, 1997.

31 Judy Dempsey, "Israel Urged to Trade Land for Peace," *Financial Times*, November 19, 1997.

32 Steve Rodan, "Qatar Conference Urges 'Land for Peace,'" *Jerusalem Post*, November 19, 1997.

33 Arnon Gafny, "The Middle East Development Fund," in Gideon Fishelson, ed., *Economic Cooperation in the Middle East* (Boulder: Westview, 1989), pp. 167–179.

34 Secretary of State James Baker, "Foreign Policy Overview," testimony before the Senate Foreign Relations Committee (Washington: Federal News Service, February 7, 1991).

35 Shimon Peres, *The New Middle East* (New York: Henry Holt, 1993), p. 111.

36 Remarks by the president to the Jordanian parliament, White House Office of the Press Secretary, October 26, 1994. On the opposition within the U.S. government, see David Makovsky, "U.S. Not Backing Peres' Bank Plan," *Jerusalem Post*, October 11, 1994, p. 2.

37 Under Secretary of the Treasury for International Affairs Lawrence Summers, "Shared Prosperity in the Middle East: Toward a Regional Development Bank," remarks at the Middle East/North Africa Economic Summit, Casablanca, October 31, 1994. For an account of the bank that emphasizes the importance of this U.S. initiative, see Dalia Dassa Kaye, "Banking on Peace: Lessons from the Middle East Development Bank," University of California Institute on Global Conflict and Cooperation (IGCC) Policy Paper no. 43, October 1998.

38 "Casablanca Party Closes with Promise of 'New Partnership,'"*Mideast Mirror* 8, no. 211 (November 1, 1994), pp. 12–13.

39 Steven Greenhouse, "Mideast Development Bank Plans Scaled Back," *New York Times*, January 15, 1995, p. A8; and Serge Schmemann, "Mideast Leaders Talk, This Time of Business," *New York Times*, October 30, 1995.

40 "The Trouble with (and at) the Amman Conference," *Mideast Mirror* 9, no. 209 (October 30, 1995), pp. 17–23, citing an article by Fahd al-Fanek in *al-'Arab*.

41 Secretary of State Warren Christopher, "The Amman Economic Summit: Transforming the Middle East Through a Public–Private Partnership" (remarks at the Sports City Complex, Amman, Jordan, October 29, 1995), *U.S. Department of State Dispatch* 6, no. 46 (November 13, 1995), p. 825.

42 *Israel Line,* October 30, 1995, citing a report by *Davar Rishon*.

43 The charter is available online at http://www.menabank.org/.

Chapter 5

Trade and Investment

The U.S. government has sought to promote trade and investment in the Levant, both among the peace process participants and between them and outside states, as part of the overall effort to foster advancements in the peace process. These efforts began at the time of the 1991 Madrid summit and accelerated after the 1993 Oslo accords. Washington's role has been multifaceted: helping to get projects started, offering technical expertise in facilitating trade and cooperation, providing financial initiatives to make cooperation more lucrative, encouraging outside investment by Jewish and Arab Americans as well as others, and mediating disputes. In general, these efforts require far less expenditure of American funds than foreign aid does, but some do require an ongoing commitment of valuable time and energy.

The efforts made by the U.S. government can be broken down into four primary categories. First, the United States offers trade privileges, or favorable terms for products produced jointly by Israel and an Arab peace process participant. Second, it promotes trade, with the U.S. government establishing institutions and holding meetings to facilitate trade among participating states. Third, it promotes investment, which involves efforts on the part of the United States to attract members of the American and international private sectors to invest in economic development projects in regional states; the strongly implied condition is that the regional states be active in or at least supportive of the peace process. Finally, the United States attempts to overcome impediments to trade and investment caused by security and related concerns.

Each of these U.S. efforts, to the extent that it is aimed at promoting the peace process as opposed to simply fostering economic development, is based upon the logic that economic development that emerges through interaction among the parties will add strength to peace agreements. Although there is no definitive scientific measure of how specific endeavors have altered the attitudes and behaviors of regional parties with regard to the peace process, the evaluations below address whether these U.S. efforts have had any apparent affect on the road to peace. Part of this assessment in some cases includes the scale of the effort made in each initiative, and whether the level of effort was adequate in relation to the goals involved.

TRADE PRIVILEGES

Several U.S. endeavors have been designed to increase cooperation among Israelis and Arabs by giving them favorable trade terms for jointly produced goods. In other words, the United States offers trade advantages for products made jointly by Israelis and either Jordanians or Palestinians; these advantages were previously given only to projects made entirely by one or the other, rather than by both together. The goal is to encourage joint industrial parks and joint investments. So far this approach has been limited, not by the willingness of the United States to provide the trade incentives, but by the hesitation of the parties to enter into joint endeavors. The most noteworthy attempts to date—and the two covered in this section—are the Qualifying Industrial Zone (QIZ) in Irbid, Jordan, and the long-delayed Gaza Industrial Estate at the Karni crossing, near the Israel–Gaza border.

The Qualifying Industrial Zone

The first industrial zone to be officially designated as a QIZ, by agreement of the United States, Jordan, and Israel, is the Irbid industrial zone. The QIZ idea is noteworthy for having originated not with U.S. officials or with the regional governments, but with regional businesspeople. These entrepreneurs lobbied their governments to create a mechanism to make joint production as lucrative as—or more lucrative than—that carried out by either party alone. The United States was unequivocally in favor of this idea, offering to provide access to the U.S. market for regional countries working together.

Most in the Israeli and Jordanian governments also responded positively, but there was resistance. In Israel, the issue causing some hesitation was the fear of losing additional jobs. According to Israeli businesspeople and finance officials interviewed, residents of the areas in Israel hardest hit by unemployment are angry at the notion of textile factories closing in

Israel and relocating to Jordan, Egypt, or the Palestinian Authority (PA), where labor is less expensive. Yet, according to these leaders, this is not a valid issue—Israel is not a cheap labor market and does not wish to be. If these plants did not move to neighboring Arab lands, government officials and economists say, they would either close entirely or move further away, such as to Southeast Asia. At least a plant in Jordan still offers some employment opportunities to Israelis, they argue. Nonetheless, the resistance of certain special interests led to a delay in Knesset approval of the QIZ.

In Jordan, some parts of the population generally oppose normalization with Israel, and this opposition is further aggravated in this case by a suspicion that the QIZ represents Israeli exploitation of the Jordanian labor pool. This objection does not carry great weight with most policymakers, as high levels of unemployment make it hard to argue against anything that would provide a significant number of jobs for Jordanians. The Irbid QIZ already provides at least 1,200 jobs for Jordanians in a region of the country with particularly high unemployment.[1] Yet, the unofficial press in Jordan refers to the QIZ and any joint ventures with Israelis as a form of exploitation, making deals more difficult for interested Jordanian businesspeople and angering some potential Israeli partners.[2]

The resistance that exists in both countries creates a mutual desire for avoiding publicity. Businesspeople interviewed from both Israel and Jordan report that in addition to the joint projects at Irbid, which are widely discussed, a number of joint ventures are developed in secrecy to avoid negative publicity. The one businessman in Jordan who openly discusses and defends his numerous dealings with Israelis also faces hostility about it, adding incentives for other Jordanians to keep secret their business with Israel. In fact, with neither side having much to gain from widespread knowledge of their activities, the avoidance of publicity is not surprising. It does, however, create difficulties in assessing how much influence U.S. efforts have had on encouraging cooperation.

It is impossible to measure the specific political impact of the QIZ, but the Jordanian and Israeli businesspeople involved strongly believe that the experience of working together, along with the financial benefit to the large number of well-paid workers and their families, is creating a strong constituency for peace. Regardless of the hesitations of some Israelis and Jordanians, there is no real argument from a U.S. perspective to curb the QIZ idea. On the contrary, the United States has many reasons to recommend expansion of the QIZ principle and to promote additional industrial zones. The QIZ is a relatively simple, effective, and inexpensive way for the United States to encourage private sector development in Jordan, a country whose economic growth and political stability serve both the peace process and broader U.S. interests.

The Gaza Industrial Estate

The political situation between Israel and the PA is much more troubled than that between Israel and Jordan, and the level of difficulty in establishing industrial zones in the West Bank and Gaza has reflected this situation. In the Palestinian areas, industrial zones would serve an even more vital purpose than they do in Jordan. They would provide the locals with employment and trade opportunities that would be virtually immune both from closures instituted by Israel in response to terrorist threats and attacks and from other border-crossing complications. Thus, the United States has been active in encouraging the establishment of industrial zones in the Palestinian areas, but progress has been slow and hard-won. Former Israeli prime minister Shimon Peres's vision of establishing twenty to thirty industrial zones in the West Bank and Gaza has been downsized to one or two zones struggling to get started.

The Gaza Industrial Estate (GIE) was the product of a U.S.–Israel–PA agreement in January 1996. Planners projected that the GIE would provide up to 20,000 jobs directly and an additional 40,000 indirectly over the long term. The goal was also for this project to serve as a prototype for a number of other industrial estates in the West Bank and Gaza and to symbolize the idea that the Palestinian areas are "open for business." When U.S. Agency for International Development (USAID) director Christopher Crowley spoke at the ceremony starting construction of the GIE, on November 15, 1996, he cited peace as the underlying goal:

> It has always been clear that the success of the peace process hinges on the ability to meet difficult economic, as well as political, challenges. Chief among these has been the necessity to promote private sector investment and employment in the West Bank and Gaza.[3]

Funding to construct and develop the GIE was forthcoming from the United States, the World Bank, and a variety of countries (including Israel). The United States pledged $6 million to develop the GIE.[4] The World Bank announced in July 1997 that it was earmarking $10 million to devote to the GIE once the security arrangements were worked out; in January 1998, although final security arrangements were not yet agreed upon, the bank approved a loan for that amount to help pay for the construction of the estate.[5] Israel itself pledged $7.5 million toward construction.

The private sector has been responsive to the idea of doing business in the GIE. Palestine Development and Investment Company (PADICO) director Amin Haddad reported that by February 1998, half of the space for twenty-two factories, which were to be available in the first phase of the project, had already been contracted by Palestinians and by joint Israeli–Palestinian ventures.[6] Ten Israeli companies, primarily in the textile field, were included. The promise of a qualified, inexpensive labor pool, guaranteed infrastructure benefits, tax deferrals for at least five (and possibly ten) years, and favorable terms for selling products to the U.S. market apparently tipped the scales for a substantial number of potential investors.

Yet, many potential Israeli investors—including the Delta Galil company, which is involved in ventures in Jordan and Egypt—remain hesitant to open businesses in the GIE, not because of security concerns but for reasons of taxation. The tax incentives offered by the PA are erased for Israelis, who are required to make up the tax benefit in payments to the Israeli authorities. There is also the continuing problem of "accumulation" in rules of origin; the European Union (EU) will not grant tax benefits that it normally offers to Israeli and Palestinian exporters if the product is made partly in the West Bank or Gaza and partly in Israel.[7]

Despite success in gaining the funding to build the site and in finding businesses to lease space there, the GIE opening was delayed by the failure of the PA and Israel to agree on security and access arrangements. Israel maintained its right to three "principles" for security: inspection by Israelis, inspection within Israeli territory, and inspection according to Israeli regulations. Whereas Israel had invested money in the GIE and expressed support for it, these security requirements made it difficult not only to conclude an agreement but also to assure potential investors that their businesses could succeed.

The U.S. administration has tried to minimize the business damages caused by security inspections by providing high-technology solutions. The United States paid for eight sophisticated cargo x-ray machines to be placed at the new terminal built on the Israeli side of the Karni crossing. These fifty-ton machines will help to screen trucks without drivers having to unload them, thereby reducing time and costs of transport that result from security measures; four of the eight machines had been placed at the terminal by the time the GIE opened for business.[8] Even after the basic security questions had been resolved, however, political complications and calculations prevented the agreement from being completed, questions remained as to immunity of the GIE from closures, and potential investors were left to wonder if their businesses would be able to function normally.

In addition to disagreements about security arrangements, a more fundamental issue arose: whether to proceed with economic cooperation initiatives while the main political issues were deadlocked. Palestinians accused Israelis of completing deals on side issues like the GIE in an attempt to distract the international community from Israel's failure to agree to a further redeployment, and the Israelis accused the PA of delaying, for purposes of political posturing, a project that could have great benefits to the Palestinian economy.

U.S. officials were involved in trying to overcome these political hurdles throughout the two years that the GIE was in the negotiation phase. Although the agreement took longer than might have been desired, each breakthrough was in large part the product of American efforts, as was the ultimate achievement of an agreement. The initial decision to establish an industrial estate near the Karni crossing was the product of a U.S.–Israeli–Palestinian agreement in January 1996. After a long period of difficulty, Secretary of State Madeleine Albright and Special Middle East Coordinator Dennis Ross made substantial progress during their respective pre–Wye summit trips to the region. During Secretary Albright's visit, the three parties agreed on the substance of the GIE arrangement, which reportedly included an agreement by Israel to allow the Palestinians to ship goods through Karni even during a closure. Yet, Albright and Netanyahu made clear after their meeting that this agreement and others reached on interim issues during their three-way discussions in Gaza would not be implemented until an overall "peace package" was concluded at the upcoming Wye summit.[9]

By the time of the Wye summit in mid-October 1998, little work remained to be done on the GIE issue, and it came as no surprise that the Wye River Memorandum included a statement that "The Israeli and Palestinian sides have agreed on arrangements which will permit the timely opening of the Gaza Industrial Estate." The tremendous U.S. political efforts that led to the Wye agreement clearly allowed the GIE arrangements to be finalized. The centrality of U.S. efforts for this project was further illustrated when the next steps in opening the GIE for business, establishing a water plant and a ceremonial ribbon-cutting, were planned around the visits of U.S. officials in December 1998.

TRADE PROMOTION

In most regions, trade among neighbors is natural and makes up a fairly large percentage of the trade activity of each state. In the Middle East, however, intraregional trade is unusually low. Despite the anti-Israeli rhetoric coming from some Arab sources, political hostility toward Israelis is not the cause of this phenomenon; trade is low even among the various Arab states. Given these circumstances, efforts to promote trade among Israel and Arabs, and indirectly among Palestinians and their Arab neighbors, have focused largely on mitigating barriers to such trade.[10] The political hostilities and the ever-changing status of the peace process have further complicated an endeavor that would have been challenging in any event. To overcome the barriers, political and otherwise, the U.S. government began a variety of initiatives designed to encourage both communication among parties and better financial and political policies. The first initiative to be discussed in this section, the Taba initiative, was a specific attempt to address those issues. The second effort described in this section, the attempt to reduce trade barriers between the parties, is less of a formal program and more of an ongoing process U.S. officials have undertaken at a variety of levels as part of their role in facilitating movement in the peace process.

The Taba Initiative

The Taba Trade Leaders Program was launched by then–Secretary of Commerce Ron Brown in February 1995. He met with the ministers of trade from Egypt, Israel, Jordan, and the PA to discuss ways of increasing trade among themselves, as well as between them and the United States. At the conclusion of that event, the participants produced the Taba Declaration, which expressed support for the peace process and for efforts to end the Arab League–sponsored boycott of Israel. The Taba participants also launched a market access study to identify trade barriers and pledged to eliminate them. Based on the results of that study, they established multilateral working groups to address specific trade issues, including quality standards and other perceived nontariff barriers.

The bilateral aspect of the Taba initiative heightened its appeal to regional states. After the 1995 Taba group meeting, Jordanians were enthusiastic about discussions of U.S. plans to offer incentives to companies to encourage investment in Jordan. Debt forgiveness for Jordan was another topic raised at the meeting that was particularly attractive to Jordanians. Such "carrots" may have helped to ease the tensions that arose at the meetings among various parties with regard to their own trade relations. Yet, not all of the bilateral issues raised at the meeting were in the form of rewards. The U.S. delegation also raised certain issues from a perspective of protecting American businesspeople—issues such as intellectual property rights and tariffs on American automobiles.

For Israel and the United States, one of the most significant outcomes of the initial Taba meeting was that government officials from the Arab countries involved not only gave broad-based support to the peace process for the first time, but they also agreed to support all efforts to end the Arab boycott against Israel. This same aspect enraged those Arab states not involved in the peace process. For example, the official Libyan statement issued in response to the 1995 Taba meeting described it as a conspiracy by the United States and Israel to increase Western control over the Arabs. According to the secretariat of Libya's General People's Committee for Unity, the Taba initiative "consecrates disunity instead of unity between Arabs, to allow the Israeli enemy to be the major force leading the region."[11]

After the death of Secretary Brown, Deputy Under Secretary Judith Barnett took over the Taba group. She had to contend with the worsening political situation that made all of the issues—including the simple matter of getting the leaders together—much more difficult. The second and third meetings of the Taba ministerial group were held in conjunction with the MENA summits of 1995 and 1996. The statement that emerged from the 1996 meeting exhibited signs of frustration creeping into the process. Arab participants remained committed to the goals of cooperation, but they voiced increased concern about the burden on the Palestinians from restrictive Israeli policies.

At the 1996 meeting the ministers endorsed the agenda for the group to continue implementing the items included in the market access study, but by the time of the 1997 MENA conference in Doha, two of the regional parties were boycotting because of peace process problems and no further meeting took place. Any success in keeping the group from totally and officially disbanding once the political climate worsened must be credited to the persistence of Judith Barnett, according to those interviewed for this study. Regional parties joke fondly about the way Barnett has insisted that they interact at least through conference calls when a meeting is not feasible. Yet, even this American determination has not brought about a meeting of the group or maintained it as a serious force in improving trade relations among the parties. In the post-Wye period, according to one Commerce official, the Commerce Department remains committed to holding another Taba group meeting, and all of the core parties except for Egypt have expressed a willingness to participate. True to the principal that normalization cannot precede bilateral progress despite the benefits it may have for all the parties, Egypt has predicated its willingness to attend another Taba gathering on further progress in implementing the Wye River agreements.

Trade Barriers

The two parties most frequently accused of imposing trade barriers that impede intraregional business are Israel and Egypt. Israelis interviewed accuse Egypt of imposing nontariff barriers (NTBs) to limit trade between Israel and Egypt. Many of these Israeli officials and businesspeople see Egypt as the primary "spoiler" in regional integration. In response, some Egyptians the authors interviewed argue that Egypt is famous for its NTBs, and that Israel is simply more sensitive to them than the many other countries affected.

Egyptian officials and business leaders interviewed also claim that the barriers come from the bottom-up rather than being imposed on the public by the government. Several Egyptians noted that if an Egyptian factory-owner wanted to import raw materials from Israel—items that he could get more cheaply from an Israeli supplier than from anywhere else—he would likely be precluded from doing so because his workers would go on strike. Public anger at Israel can be so intense that, even if a businessperson respects a particular Israeli individual as a supporter of the peace process, doing business with that Israeli would be too costly in terms of public relations. Not all Israelis interviewed, however, accept this explanation. They believe the Egyptian government is sending messages to businesspeople not to deal with Israel, and they would like to see the United States put more pressure on Egypt to remove barriers to trading with Israel. Israelis cite examples of official harassment of Israelis doing business in Cairo as proof of the governmental source of resistance. They are frustrated by the "cold peace" with Egypt and do not accept the political stalemate between Israel and other regional parties as justification for holding up normalization.

Yet, even as Israelis accuse Egypt of erecting trade barriers to prevent business ties to Israel, other parties admonish Israel for using NTBs to defend its own protectionist interests. One example is the issue of safety standards for products. Israelis claim that the standards are not intended as a barrier, but on the contrary are an example of treating Palestinian and Jordanian producers as equals. One aspect of the problem, the expense for Jordanians of sending a sample product to the Israeli standards inspector for testing, was resolved early in 1998, when the Israeli and Jordanian standards authorities agreed to test for each other's standards. This resolution came as a result of bilateral talks, illustrating that the desire and the political climate to resolve trade issues is often more of a decisive factor in overcoming difficulties than is the offer of technical assistance by the United States and other outside parties.

The Palestinians, Jordanians, and Egyptians all criticize Israel for using the pretext of security concerns to keep Palestinians as a captive market and to avoid competition for Israeli producers. Israelis are divided between those who agree with this assessment, and others who are adamant that all of the measures are in fact necessary for security. The potential for U.S. assistance lies in finding areas in which barriers can be lowered without compromising security. U.S. officials can then encourage Israel to relax those barriers and can offer technical assistance in making the transitions.

Most of the problems are resolvable through mutual agreements. It is noteworthy, however, that both Jordan and the Palestinians look at the difference between the sizes of their economies and that of Israel, and claim that Israel should be more magnanimous in forming agreements with these two entities. They point out the favorable agreements Israel initially received from larger, more established trading partners like Europe and the United States.

The trade barriers that draw the most ire from the Arab parties are those imposed by Israel that limit trade not between Israel and Egypt or Jordan, but rather between either of those two Arab states and the Palestinians. The PA is also angry at Israeli measures that make it difficult for the Palestinians to trade with parties outside the region. In that regard, U.S. offers to provide technological and practical solutions to security issues can be useful, as can U.S. efforts to promote agreements on interim issues such as the Gaza airport and seaport, which would enable the Palestinians to conduct trade more independently.

The U.S. efforts in tackling trade barriers, primarily through offers of logistical assistance, contrast strongly with the European approach of using threats in an attempt to influence Israeli policy. The EU has threatened to penalize Israeli products made in the West Bank and Gaza and the Golan, arguing that they are not technically entitled to the status of "Made in Israel." They have been open about their real motivation to induce a change in Israeli policy toward Palestinian trade with outsiders. They insist that Israel should make it easier for the Palestinians to trade with partners other than Israel itself. Although the EU sees this approach as the most effective way to influence Israeli policy, the United States has avoided such strong-arming. To the extent that Israeli restrictions are protectionist rather than security-oriented, trade threats do offer a powerful tool for persuasion. Yet, if the ultimate concern is the peace process, such techniques on the part of the United States could have the potential to backfire. The Israeli resistance to pressure by the United States could cause tensions between the two that would make Israelis more hesitant to move ahead with the peace process.

INVESTMENT AND DEVELOPMENT PROMOTION

Just as the Middle East has been slow in building trade among regional parties, it has also had difficulty in attracting outside economic ties. Several U.S. initiatives have sought to foster the peace process by encouraging an increased flow of foreign investment into regional states as an indirect "peace dividend." As with trade promotion, these efforts have been hampered by the fact that the lack of peace was far from the only factor inhibiting foreign investment. To the extent that certain regional states, like Jordan and Egypt, reformed their economic policies to become more attractive to investors, the United States could help draw attention to these countries and their positive changes. Insofar as political conditions still made potential investors wary, the United States could try to help with risk insurance. Yet, the U.S. government is ultimately limited in the influence it can exert over the choices of private sector companies. Realizing that concerns such as corruption, unpredictable or unstable investment laws, political instability, and a lack of transparency are of primary importance to companies, the United States has sought to address these issues as well as simply trying to attract and convince companies to invest.

One of the programs discussed in this section, Builders for Peace, involves a direct U.S. attempt to draw foreign private sector money into the Palestinian economy. Another, the Middle East Regional Cooperation Program (MERC), is an initiative that actually earmarks U.S. government funding for scientific projects that involve Israel and at least one Arab party. The final topic covered in this section, Palestinian corruption, is different in that, rather than discussing a direct attempt to infuse public or private sector money into the Palestinian economy, it deals with one of the underlying causes of difficulty in actually bringing investment money to the PA areas.

Builders for Peace

Builders for Peace (hereafter, "Builders") is one of the few U.S. economic initiatives whose failure has become undeniable and undebatable. An examination of the history of Builders is particularly instructive for this study because of what one official involved refers to as the chasm between theory and practice: Everyone initially supported the project—and then participated in defeating it. It is also useful because the rise and fall of Builders, with all of the credit and blame that can be generously distributed, illustrates what can happen when high-level officials do not step in to shield the political goals from economic bureaucracy, and the economic goals from the fluctuations of Arab–Israeli politics.

Conceived during the euphoria of the signing of the Oslo accords, Builders was launched at the White House during a celebratory lunch for Arab and Jewish Americans. President Clinton proposed at that meeting that this group of prominent Americans with respective ties to the two sides in the Arab–Israeli conflict could help the peace process by working together to jump-start the Palestinian economy with foreign investment. Vice President Al Gore then became the administration official most closely identified with putting together the team. The executive director, Joseph DeSutter, came from Gore's foreign policy staff.

The idea was received with enthusiasm not only by the leaders present at that White House gathering, but also by the Palestinian and Israeli governments and regional businesspeople. Builders seemed like a no-lose proposition: American businesspeople would have an opportunity to profit in a new arena, with the cushion of significant risk insurance. Arab and Jewish American leaders would put their differences aside and acquire a stake in the peace process. Palestinians would get much-needed investment to bolster their economy and address the issue of unemployment. All of these elements would undoubtedly be helpful to the peace process.

There is no shortage of theories for why Builders, after enjoying such auspicious beginnings, failed. Some of the reasons were as follows:

Lack of High-Level U.S. Commitment: The Overseas Private Investment Corporation (OPIC), a U.S. government corporation, pledged to provide insurance for the private investors Builders attracted to the region. OPIC initially pledged $125 million for the West Bank and Gaza over five years, but much of it was never awarded. A statement by an OPIC official cited the corporation's need to make sure its projects all demonstrate commercial viability, but this approach ignored the particular political agenda and needs that spawned Builders. One Builders insider interviewed faults U.S. officials for treating economic initiatives as a lower priority than political matters, arguing that the U.S. government should have used its influence to mitigate the damage of unproductive Israeli and Palestinian approaches to specific projects. Involvement at the highest U.S. political levels was necessary to protect Builders from OPIC criteria that ignored peace-related goals, as well as from other bureaucratic hurdles. But the failure by high-level officials to intervene in that way left Builders at a disadvantage from the start.

Habitual Hostility: The Jewish and Arab American communities each had a leader co-presiding over Builders; Mel Levine, a former Democratic congressman from California, and James Zogby, president of the Arab–American Institute, respectively. According to one professional involved in Builders, they were honorary leaders more than active participants. It was helpful to have a prestigious member of each community to lend credibility to the project, but choosing political leaders rather than commercial figures to serve as copresidents set the tone for Arab–Israeli politics overshadowing economic possibilities. Further, one interview subject close to Builders notes that Zogby's tendency to make remarks criticizing Israel, and the

THE GAZA BUSINESS CENTER AND MARRIOTT HOTEL

By far the most ambitious project associated with Builders was the Gaza Business Center and Marriott Hotel. The plans for the center included a 300-room hotel and associated facilities which, it was hoped, would employ 600 people directly and 4,000 indirectly, contributing $50 million a year to the Gaza economy. The owners were to include General Resources Design Group (GRDG), based in Virginia, in conjunction with DigiCell Corporation; Hughes Network Systems, a subsidiary of General Motors; the PA; and Salam International Investments of Qatar.

Early in the planning of the business center, Ziad Karram, the main force behind the project, credited Builders with playing an important role in getting the project off the ground. He thanked them for providing access to the U.S. government and to OPIC. Ironically, by the time of the dedication ceremony on March 3, 1997, when the center was dedicated to the late Commerce Secretary Ron Brown, it had become clear that OPIC insurance would not be available after all.

OPIC officials made their funding decisions not on the basis of the politicians' hopes, but on their assessment of financial feasibility, and a sophisticated business center in an area that hardly has a sewage system was suspect in its prospects. While promising a certain amount of money in OPIC insurance for businesses investing in the West Bank and Gaza, the U.S. government did not resolve the inherent contradiction between its peace goals and OPIC's selection criteria. Construction began on the Gaza Business Center, but the project remains far from completed owing to a lack of funds. This long-time symbol of the potential for economic development in Gaza, and the potential for U.S. investment promotion efforts, now serves as an ironic reminder of the limitations in both regards.

Jewish members' proclivity to circulate accounts of these statements (even when taken out of context), created a great deal of tension and division among the Jewish and Arab leadership bases.

Terrorism, Israeli Security Measures, and Protectionism: As discussed elsewhere in this chapter, acts of terrorism by Palestinians who reject the peace process have led Israel to institute border closures, and this makes investment much less appealing. Some critics, including a number of Israelis, argue that the security measures Israel takes sometimes go beyond what is necessary and enter the realm of protectionism and/or collective punishment. Either way, closures made Builders' task of attracting private investors to the West Bank and Gaza much more challenging.

Palestinian Corruption: The problem of corruption in PA business practices is also discussed in a separate section of this chapter, as it affected not only Builders but all attempts to bring outside investors to the West Bank and Gaza.

According to Levine and Zogby, it would not be fair to say that Builders accomplished nothing. Both men told the Associated Press that Builders had at least one positive outcome, as it was the first time the Arab and Jewish communities in the United States worked together.[12] Unfortunately, more tangible benefits like completed projects and the jobs they would bring proved elusive, leaving an array of dashed hopes.

The Middle East Regional Cooperation (MERC) Program

The MERC program, a product of the Camp David accords, was established by Congress in 1979 as part of an economic interaction program designed to promote scientific cooperation between Egypt and Israel.[13] Congressman Harry Waxman (D-Calif.) sponsored a bill that allocated $5 million of the USAID budget for a trilateral research program that focuses on applying technology to solve timely regional problems dealing with agriculture, water resources, and health. After the Oslo accords and the Jordanian–Israeli Peace Treaty, Morocco, Jordan, Tunisia, Lebanon, and the Palestinian Authority joined MERC. Funding for the program, as part of the USAID budget, is reviewed on an annual basis by Congress. From 1979 to 1990, funding was $5 million a year; in 1990, it was increased to $7 million a year, with $5 million sustaining ongoing projects and $2 million supporting U.S., Israeli, and Palestinian cooperation in developing the West Bank and Gaza.[14] Since 1990, the level of annual funding has remained unchanged.

An assessment of MERC's twenty years shows a modest but significant set of tangible benefits tempered by political problems. Projects funded have focused on palpable issues such as waste-water management, containing coastline erosions, desalinating and rerouting rivers, and researching infectious diseases.[15] Additionally, the laboratories of Palestinian universities have been modernized, and students are able to do more substantial research. In addition to these scientific achievements, there has been some modest success in fostering people-to-people contact and exchanges.

To a limited extent, MERC funding has created "solid professional ties and eased communication" between Arabs and Israelis by serving as a conduit for the region's scientists to meet their counterparts for the first time, by reducing stereotypes, and by forming professional and personal relationships.[16] Tangible scientific successes lead to a better working atmosphere within the region and facilitate a warmer peace. For example, based on fifteen years of beneficial agricultural cooperation, Egypt's Ministry of Agriculture has become a staunch supporter of normalized relations with Israel. In another case, Hebrew University cell biologist Abraham Hochberg calls his cancer research project, run jointly by Israelis and Palestinians, "science, cancer diagnosis, and peace together."[17]

Unfortunately, most of the research projects are actually "parallel" investigations that do not entail frequent partnership. Scientists work on similar problems separately and then exchange advice and views with each other. Moreover, only a limited number of scientists and coordinators are involved in these workshops; lower-level scientists and staff are usually excluded from regional meetings. In eighteen projects over twenty years, more than $100 million has been spent for fewer than 100 different scientists to have contact with each other.[18] This seems like a high price for a small amount of interaction, if one of MERC's main goals is to increase personal ties and normalization.

In addition to a structure that inadvertently minimizes direct contacts, the success of MERC has been limited by several political problems. Egyptian and Palestinian scientists have both shown reluctance to work publicly with Israeli scientists. Arab scientists fear that publishing a study with Israelis or even working with them will damage their reputations in the Arab world, causing them to be excluded from future lucrative job opportunities in Saudi Arabia and Kuwait.[19] This fear of stigmatization will exist as long as political hostility is present in the region.

Moreover, as Egypt can acquire most of the technology involved in such projects from European sources, the political risks of dealing with Israel do not always seem worthwhile. This reluctance has made the U.S.

role invaluable—at MERC's inception, the United States was involved in bilateral dealings with each country. Over time, the United States has been able to achieve trilateral and multilateral agreements with the regional actors, but the role of U.S. involvement as manager and facilitator has remained critical.[20]

PA Corruption

Certain disadvantages are inherent in being a brand new entity of indeterminate status, with limited but densely populated land and even more limited water resources. Yet, these unavoidable problems, combined with the restrictions imposed by Israel on the PA, are not the full story of economic woes in the West Bank and Gaza, and particularly of the difficulties in attracting investment. Another piece to the puzzle is mismanagement and corruption within the PA. A report by the PA comptroller issued in May 1997 alleged that the Palestinians had lost $326 million in 1996 owing to mismanagement and misuse of funds. This triggered an investigation by a PLC investigative committee, which produced a sixty-page report that included specific allegations of corruption on the part of very high-level PA officials and demanded that PA chairman Yasir Arafat dismiss his entire cabinet.[21] Even a source as unlikely as Arafat's wife has alleged publicly that he is "surrounded by corrupt people," particularly his advisers, who tarnish Arafat's image by engaging in corruption and dishonesty.[22] This image is widely shared among Palestinians and foreigners, leaving potential private-sector investors wary of the same lack of transparency, tendency toward monopolies, and bloated bureaucracy that make some donor countries hesitant to fulfill their obligations to the PA. Similar concerns constrain potential private sector investors, including diaspora Palestinians.

Arafat is taken to task domestically for corruption, and a few of the most popular and well-respected members of the Palestinian Authority and the Palestinian Legislative Council (PLC) have resigned over just this issue. In 1997, Haidar Abd al-Shafi resigned from the PLC because of corruption in the PA and the failure of the PLC to do anything about it. In 1998, Hanan Ashrawi resigned from Arafat's cabinet because of Arafat's failure to make substantive changes to resolve corruption issues in the PA. When she declined a position in Arafat's enlarged (as opposed to reconstituted) cabinet, she explained, "We had been promised reform and a system of accountability, transparency, that there would be investigations and that the rule of law would be upheld. Those pledges were not met, and the real issues were not addressed."[23]

Some Israelis interviewed complain that, whereas U.S. officials have put tremendous pressure on Israel to ease conditions for the Palestinians, they have not used their leverage over or influence on the PA to encourage or demand better governance. Yet, the U.S. government faces a complex task in trying to mitigate Palestinian corruption. One widely held belief is that Arafat, although far from perfect, is a better choice and more likely to achieve peace with Israel than any other potential Palestinian leader. On that basis, the United States hesitates to act in ways that might undermine Arafat's authority or exacerbate his extensive domestic political problems. When Arafat appears to be ineffective or too much under the influence of the United States, he loses popularity to more extreme forces like the Islamic group Hamas. For the United States, the potential gain in investment money for the Palestinians if corruption issues were resolved is not worth any loss of power by the one man deemed most likely and most able to make peace with Israel.

OVERCOMING SECURITY CONCERNS

The connection between the peace process and economic development does not have the same level of urgency for all the parties involved. For the Palestinians more than any other party, peace, politics, and economics are intricately bound together and viewed less in terms of prosperity than in terms of simple survival. For the Israelis, economic gains might be a nice side benefit from the peace process, but the primary goal is security—not simply national security in military terms, about which many Israelis feel confident—but personal security of individual Israelis from terrorist attacks. Yet, ironically, incidences of terror attacks against Israelis (and political violence among Israelis) increased rather than decreased in the years following Oslo. Progress in the peace process increases the desperation of extremists who oppose it, and for opponents such as Hamas, terrorist attacks became the chosen method not only to demonstrate opposition to the peace process, but also to seek to derail it.

For U.S. officials seeking to advance the peace process, it is natural to be both against terrorism and in favor of Palestinian economic development. Yet, these interests often seem to conflict. When Israel implements measures designed to enhance the security of Israeli citizens, those measures by definition include restraints on the freedom of Palestinian residents of the West Bank and Gaza. To further complicate matters, the Palestinians have made a convincing argument in certain instances that measures described by Israel as security precautions are really unnecessary for that purpose, and are actually serving protectionist purposes for Israeli industries—or are simply punitive. Even among different elements of the Israeli government, there are disputes over the extent to which all of the measures described as "security" measures are actually necessary. U.S. officials have taken on the delicate task of seeking to mitigate the economic damages to the Palestinians, without directly challenging Israel's judgment of its own security needs. The particular measures the U.S. government has become involved in are closures of the borders, "safe passage" for Palestinians between Gaza and the West Bank, and the establishment of the Gaza International Airport.

Closures

Closures are one of the most controversial issues in Israeli–Palestinian relations. They involve Israeli limitations on people and goods entering or leaving the West Bank and Gaza, ranging from chronic border restrictions to the total closures that follow terrorist attacks in Israel. Israel's justification for the closures is security, with closures touted as a way to protect Israeli citizens from Palestinians who might enter Israel with the intent to launch terrorist attacks. From the Palestinian perspective, closures are a form of collective punishment. Their effect is to choke the Palestinian economy by preventing imports and exports, and by limiting the ability of workers to cross into Israel for jobs that had long provided crucial income to the Palestinian economy. In 1996, closures cost the West Bank economy an estimated $500.9 million, and Gaza, another $461.1 million.[24]

Some Palestinians argue that Gaza and the West Bank have, since the 1991 Gulf War, been continuously under some degree of closure.[25] Yet, distinctions are useful, as the degree of restriction and, therefore, of economic damage varies greatly. Closures can affect Gaza without involving the West Bank. They can include exceptions for various categories of people to cross; even during total closures, certain categories of workers may be permitted to enter Israel. Certain restrictions seem to be reasonably related to security concerns, whereas others are presumably matters of punishment or protectionism. One type of closure that has been applied occasionally—internal closure—prevents movement of people and goods between different areas of the West Bank. Israel has justified this by claiming that it is necessary for capturing terrorists who have just committed attacks,[26] but Palestinians see it as further evidence that the aim of closures is more for punishment than security. For instance, closures can include shutting down the pipeline that brings natural gas into Gaza from Israel. As it is not feasible to smuggle any solid object through that line, there is no plausible security reason for shutting it. Similarly, closures often extend to the pipe at the Gaza–Israel border crossing through which dry cement mix is blown. That pipe has in it a fine mesh grating that prevents any extraneous object from passing through. In this case, a system designed precisely to address security concerns (that is, to allow inspections of dry cement mix) is nevertheless shut down during closures, suggesting that the motive is as much punishment as it is preventing terrorism.

The Israeli government justifies closures that have followed terrorist incidents as preventing follow-up attacks and facilitating the search for the attackers. Other closures have been preventive, planned for times seen as likely to inspire terrorism—Jewish or Muslim holidays, Israeli or Palestinian celebrations, and periods following suspected Israeli action against Hamas activists. The likelihood of imposing closures as a response to events has also varied with changes in the Israeli government. Whereas the Labor government was more amenable to the principle of territorial compromise than its successor Likud government has been, the Likud government has been more committed to avoiding closures and to facilitating the entrance of Palestinian laborers into Israel. The number of days of closure rose steadily from 1993 to 1996, and then dropped in 1997.[27]

Israeli prime minister Binyamin Netanyahu has claimed that the decreases in closures are because of his government's commitment to Palestinian economic development and his understanding that alleviating Palestinian poverty is an Israeli interest.[28] In addition, closures may be unappealing to a Likud government because they revive the 1967 "Green Line" between Israel and the territories that Likud leaders would like to de-emphasize.[29] An opinion piece by Haggai Huberman in the nationalist Israeli newspaper *Hatzofeh* makes this point about the idea of building a border fence between Israel and the West Bank: It would, says Huberman, "constitute a revival of the Green Line, precisely by a Likud government, 30 years after it was erased in the Six Day War."[30] Whatever the reason for the decrease in closures—a trend that continued in 1998—it did result in positive economic trends for the West Bank and Gaza, including a decrease in unemployment, an increase in the number of workers employed in Israel (both legally and illegally), and a rise in the gross national product (GNP).[31] Nevertheless, the economic situation of the Palestinians was much worse in 1998 than in 1993; the improvements in 1997–1998 did not make up for the deterioration in 1994–1996.

In addition to resenting the economic hardships caused by closures, most Palestinians do not accept the logic of closures as a means to enhance Israeli security. They see it, rather, as a form of collective punishment for acts of terrorism and a card Israel holds over the heads of the PA. Hassan Asfour, the PA coordinator of negotiations with Israel, argued on Egyptian radio that closures are clearly not for security because Palestinian workers do not commit violations while in Israel, and "the operations that took place before were carried out using means that cannot be prevented by any closure." He argues that closures are "actually a political action that is targeting the Palestinians and aims to apply pressure on the Palestinian leadership to give in to more concessions. . ." [32]

Even among the Israeli security establishment, disagreement exists over whether prolonged closures help or hurt Israel's security.[33] The argument that they may even damage Israel's security is based on the belief, not universally accepted, that a major factor in the motivation for terrorism is the despair brought about by unemployment and general economic hopelessness. According to Huberman, the Israeli police and central command supported the continuation of a lengthy closure in the late summer of 1998 to prevent against explicitly threatened Hamas attacks. The Israeli General Security Services and the bureau of the coordinator for government activities in the territories disputed this claim, however, for they believed that by increasing unemployment and desperation, prolonged closures actually add to the strength and appeal of the very Hamas institutions that Israel is trying to weaken.[34]

U.S. officials have been attempting to mitigate the damage closures do to the Palestinian economy and psyche, without asking Israel to compromise on security considerations. This U.S. position is based on a belief, shared by many Israelis and virtually all Arabs, that Israel's security concerns can be addressed more constructively and in a way that is less restrictive for Palestinians. U.S. contributions to Israeli security have included offering technology that would make inspections easier; sending an embassy representative to border crossings to mediate on a day-to-day basis; and urging the Israelis to provide more VIP passes and other exceptions to the closures.

U.S. embassy officials have also been sympathetic to the humiliation suffered by Palestinians using the crossing points. A report issued by the U.S. embassy in Tel Aviv in September 1996 describes indignities experienced at the Erez crossing by a U.S. official and a prominent Palestinian businessman who had been granted a VIP pass. The report expresses frustration at the treatment of well-known Palestinians, and it raises the question of how less-well-connected Palestinians were faring at the crossings. The report concludes by pointing out the damaging effect that "gratuitous humiliation" causes among the Palestinians.

Palestinian Authority officials view U.S. efforts in this matter quite positively. Some believe that only the United States has any potential to ease their plight in any way, and they appreciate the efforts of the U.S. embassy official who comes from Tel Aviv to checkpoints, sometimes on a daily basis, to deal with closure questions. They are also grateful for the technology the United States has offered, including x-ray machines, to make the border crossing points more efficient. Yet, Palestinians wish the Americans would apply more direct pressure on Israel to ease closures. Some Israeli finance officials, whose belief that a better Palestinian standard of living would ultimately benefit Israel leads them to urge the security forces to ease restrictions where possible, are also grateful for the U.S. efforts.

The U.S. efforts to ease closures positively influence the peace negotiations by improving Arabs' view of Americans as impartial mediators. Seeing U.S. officials take a position on the Palestinians' behalf in relation to the Israelis helps Arabs to view the United States as an even-handed honest broker, rather than first and foremost as an Israeli advocate. There are undoubtedly times when this improved image has provided U.S. officials with increased clout in convincing Palestinian officials to attend or remain in a negotiating session, to compromise on a particular issue, or to accept a strategic proposal. Furthermore, this benefit is achieved without confronting the Israelis on what they see as core issues, like territorial concessions.

'Safe Passage'

"Safe Passage" is a shorthand phrase for one of the issues slated to be settled during the interim period of the Oslo accords. The term refers to the ability of Palestinians to travel and transport goods between the West Bank and Gaza. For the Palestinians, this is a matter of practical concern for personal and economic issues, as well as a symbolic matter of feeling like one political unit. Israel has hesitated to conclude an agreement to open a land route between the West Bank and Gaza, generally citing security concerns based on the need to cross into Israeli territory.

U.S. officials have been sympathetic to the desire of Palestinians to have direct, open, and free transportation between the West Bank and Gaza, as well as to Israel's concerns about security. Under Secretary of State Stuart Eizenstat informed an Israeli audience that Palestinian entrepreneurs have complained to him about spending more to ship goods from the West Bank to Gaza than from the West Bank to Venice.[35] This prevents businesses in either area from having access to half of their natural market. The high costs of transport also compel the Palestinians in many cases to purchase more expensive Israeli products, which are brought in more easily. Palestinians are thus left with the impression that the refusal to provide access between the West Bank and Gaza is more accurately a matter of protectionism than of security concerns. Adding to this impression of protectionism is the set of restrictions making it difficult and expensive for Palestinians to import goods from Jordan and Egypt, which would also be less expensive for Palestinian consumers but would cut into the Israeli market.

U.S. negotiators have made an effort to encourage an agreement on West Bank–Gaza passage routes, and the progress made to date has largely been a product of U.S. intervention. The mid-1998 U.S.-sponsored negotiations got stuck as Israel insisted on certain security precautions and the Palestinians refused infringements on their autonomy.[36] U.S. officials and Palestinian negotiators hoped to conclude a definitive agreement at Wye in October 1998, but disagreements over the types of vehicles to use on passage routes complicated the issue. The following language is included in the Wye River Memorandum with regard to this item:

> Both sides will renew negotiations on Safe Passage immediately. As regards the southern route, the sides will make best efforts to conclude the agreement within a week of the entry into force of this Memorandum. Operation of the southern route will start as soon as possible thereafter. As regards the northern route, negotiations will continue with the goal of reaching agreement as soon as possible. Implementation will take place expeditiously thereafter.[37]

Several months after the Wye summit, however, agreement on opening land transport routes continued to be delayed. Like many elements of the accord, it appeared to be held up by conflict over central issues between the parties. U.S. officials have persisted in calling for implementation of safe passage, along with the rest of Wye.

Gaza International Airport
One of the most noteworthy achievements of the October 1998 Wye Memorandum, and indeed of U.S. economic efforts in the peace process, was the opening of the Gaza International Airport in November 1998. The airport had been an important matter for the Palestinians since before Arafat even arrived in Gaza, for both practical and symbolic reasons. Agreement-in-principle to build the airport was reached within the negotiations for the Interim Agreement (Oslo II) signed in September 1995, and the airport was originally scheduled to open in May 1996. When the original time-

table was not met, the airport was then included in the January 1997 Hebron "Note for the Record" as an item under the list of "Israeli items for negotiation," and from then until the Wye summit the two sides talked about arrangements for opening the airport but did not reach a conclusion.

By the time of the Wye summit the airport had long been ready for operations, and it was clear that the extensive delay in opening the airport was because of disagreements between the sides on a range of issues focusing on security precautions but also including symbolic matters such as the name of the airport. [38] In terms of security, Israel feared that, without extensive Israeli security control over the airport's operation, the facility could serve as a conduit for weapons and illegal entrants. Palestinians worried that the Israeli security demands were so stringent that they would strangle the airport and relegate it to being, in the words of Palestinian official Yasir Abd Rabbuh, "a mere decoration." [39] For a long time, each side rejected many of the other side's proposals about security and administration. By the end of 1997, however, virtually all of the substantive matters had been resolved, using some high-tech solutions as well as a number of artful compromises. It then became apparent that the impasse in the airport's opening was because of political factors, not disagreements over security concerns.

The political factors related largely to a rare area of agreement between the Israeli government and the PA: Both saw the airport not only as an opportunity for the Palestinians to expand their trade and commerce, and to move about more freely, but also as a powerful symbol of Palestinian sovereignty. The weight this held for both parties—eager excitement for the Palestinians and trepidation for the Israelis—stemmed from the context of the ongoing battle of words about whether the Palestinians will declare statehood unilaterally after the Oslo interim period expires. That question looms as one of the most contentious and politically explosive issues for final status talks, and both sides viewed the airport as a step in the direction as statehood. This fact was illustrated by the debate over whether President Clinton's December 1998 trip to the region would include a landing of Air Force One at the Gaza International Airport. The Palestinians were very eager for this, and the Israelis were vociferously opposed, both seeing such a landing as equivalent to U.S. recognition of Palestinian statehood. The compromise worked out was that Clinton would land at the airport not in Air Force One, but in a helicopter.

U.S. involvement was key to achieving enough understanding on these political matters to move beyond the impasse. At the Wye summit, which was called and, by all accounts nursed painstakingly along, by Clinton

Clinton and other high-level administration officials, the parties concluded a "Protocol Regarding the Establishment and Operation of the International Airport in the Gaza Strip During the Interim Period." The airport opened officially, with much fanfare—"brass bands, bagpipes, and grandiloquent speeches"—on November 24, 1998. [40] By that time the opening of the airport had been delayed for more than two years, and—without strong and direct U.S. intervention—the delay would most likely have continued indefinitely.

POLICY ISSUES

Trade and investment facilitation efforts have the desirable quality of being welcomed by, rather than imposed upon, almost all of the regional parties. They have few risks and some potential advantages even apart from the peace process. Few would advocate curtailing trade efforts; the policy decisions in this regard are primarily choices of type and degree. In other words, government decision makers must continually reevaluate which of these efforts they are prioritizing, whether the resources being devoted to them are adequate, and whether particular programs should be continued exactly as they are, altered in some way, or discontinued.

U.S. efforts have been, and can continue to be, useful in persuading those "fence-sitters" to do business in the region. Some initiatives have been helpful in moving the parties toward pragmatic solutions to particular disputes, even when the roots of the problems are political. Oftentimes, quieter, more modest undertakings, like having a representative at border crossings to mediate security issues, can be more productive than large regionwide programs. Particular initiatives are also most likely to work when the resources devoted to them are consistent and adequate, and when the U.S. officials overseeing them take a strong, continuous interest. Perhaps most important in helping the peace process is the feeling these initiatives engender among Arab parties, that the United States is looking out for their interests.

Israeli and Jordanian officials would like to see additional U.S. efforts to encourage cooperative ventures between Israel and its neighbors. A number of Israelis would like to see additional U.S. programs to encourage U.S. corporations to invest in joint trilateral programs with an Israeli and a Jordanian, Palestinian, or Egyptian company. Proponents of such plans suggest that the U.S. government could facilitate more cooperative projects between Israel and its peace partners by providing more risk insurance, or perhaps special tax benefits, for those ventures. These types of steps lack in publicity benefits and symbolic value, but may compensate for that with other dividends. A question remains, however, as to how much direct benefit these programs can have for the peace process if they do not involve parties—like Jordan and Israel—that are already predisposed toward peace.

Efforts to promote investment have indicated that such attempts, even when geared toward political results, can succeed only when they make economic sense for the investors. U.S. officials and programs are limited in their ability to influence the decision making of private-sector actors. Although tax advantages and risk insurance can help sway potential investors who are "on the fence" (if the government follows through on them), they cannot fully erase concerns about the investment climate in a particular area. Nor can they create an industrial park on the border between two sides who can barely speak to each other—not until the sides reach some political understandings can such an endeavor succeed and thus reinforce that political progress.

Notes

1. "Jordan: U.S. Officials Designate Controversial Estate as Qualified Industrial Zone," *Middle East Business Intelligence*, February 5, 1998.

2. "Jordan: Jordanian Paper on 'Apprehensions' Regarding QIZ in Irbid," *Amman al-Sabil*, March 10, 1998, p. 3, in FBIS-NES-98-070, March 11, 1998.

3. "USAID Director Christopher D. Crowley at the Ceremonial Opening of the Gaza Industrial Estate, Friday, November 16, 1996," available on the United States Information Agency web site, http://www.usia.gov/.

4. "Ambassador to Israel Indyk's Remarks on Mideast Peace," June 20, 1997, U.S. Information Agency web site, http://www.usia.gov/.

5. Jennifer Friedlin and David Harris, "World Bank Earmarks $10 Million for Gaza Industrial Park," *Jerusalem Post*, July 24, 1997. "World Bank OKs $10M Loan for Gaza," Associated Press, January 23, 1998.

6. Nina Gilbert, "Ten Firms Show Interest in Karni Park," *Jerusalem Post*, February 19, 1998.

7. Jessica Steinberg, "Kitan to Open Karni Plant in Two Weeks, Others to Follow," *Jerusalem Post*, January 11, 1999.

8. Patricia Golan, "Marketing a Hard Sell for Gaza Industrial Estate," *Jerusalem Post*, December 5, 1998.

9. David Makovsky, Yerach Tal, and Gideon Alon, "Final Status Talks Possible at Summit," *Ha'aretz* (English internet edition), October 8, 1998.

10. For a discussion of the paucity of trade among Arab states and the small role of Arab–Israeli hostilities in limiting intraregional trade, see Hisham Awartani and

Ephraim Kleiman, "Economic Interactions Among Participants in the Middle East Peace Process," *Middle East Journal* 51, no. 2 (Spring 1997), pp. 215–229.

11   "Tripoli TV: Taba Meeting Held Under 'U.S. Tutelage,'" Tripoli Libyan Television Network, February 8, 1995, in FBIS-NES-95-027, February 8, 1995, p. 23.

12   Donna Abu-Nasr, "U.S. Arab–Jewish Group Unravels as Peace Process Slows," Associated Press, August 21, 1997.

13   The authors would like to thank Washington Institute research assistant Ben Orbach for contributing this section on MERC.

14   Daniel C. Kurtzer, deputy assistant secretary of state, "Middle East Multilaterals," testimony before the House Appropriations Subcommittee on Foreign Operations (Washington: Federal Document Clearing House, May 6, 1994).

15   Zvi Hellman, "Quiet Economic Ties," *Jerusalem Post*, June 14, 1991.

16   Robert Pelletreau, "FY1996 Economic Programs for Promoting Peace on the Middle East" (statement before the Senate Foreign Relations Subcommittee on Near Eastern and South Asian Affairs, May 11, 1994), *U.S. Department of State Dispatch* 6, no. 21 (May 22, 1995).

17   Jocelyn Kaiser, "As Mideast Peace Process Lags, Science Endures," *American Association for the Advancement of Science* 279, no. 5356 (March 6, 1998), p. 1447.

18   Krishna Kumar and Irving Rosenthal, "Scientific Cooperation and Peace Building: A Case Study of USAID's Middle East Regional Cooperation Program," *USAID Evaluation Special Study* report no. 77 (April 1998), p. 31.

19   Hellman, "Quiet Economic Ties."

20   Kumar and Rosenthal, "Scientific Cooperation and Peace Building."

21   Serge Schmemann, "Corruption Panel Urges Arafat to Dismiss His Cabinet," *New York Times*, July 30, 1997, p. 3.

22   "Suha Arafat on Religious, Political Issues," *El Pais* (Spain), in FBIS-NES-98-348, December 14, 1998; the *El Pais* article was later quoted in "Suha Arafat: "My Husband is Surrounded by Corrupt People," *Ma'ariv*, December 15, 1998.

23   Ilene R. Prusher, "Why a Human Rights Advocate Leaves Arafat's Cabinet," *Christian Science Monitor*, August 31, 1998.

24   Ishac Diwan and Radwan A. Shaban, eds., "Development Under Adversity: The Palestinian Economy in Transition," (Palestine Economic Policy Research Institute [MAS] and the World Bank, 1998), p. 6.

25   Ghassan Khatib, *Palestine Report* (Eastern Jerusalem: Jerusalem Media and Communication Centre, April 16, 1998).

26   "The Entry of Palestinians to Jerusalem and Bethlehem," report by the Information Division, Israeli Foreign Ministry, December 31, 1997, online at http://www.israel-mfa.gov.il/.

27 Figures on closures from 1993 to 1996 were obtained from the summary of Diwan and Shaban, eds., "Development Under Adversity." For figures for closures in 1997, see UN Economic and Social Council, "Summary of the Survey of Economic and Social Developments in the ESCWA Region, 1997–1998," (New York: United Nations, April 17, 1998).

28 "Israeli–Palestinian Economic Relations Update," Israeli Foreign Ministry, May 25, 1998, online at http://www.israel-mfa.gov.il/.

29 "Keeping People in their Place," *Economist* online, September 15, 1998, at http://www.economist.com/editorial/justforyou/current/ir6788.html/.

30 Haggai Huberman, "A Prolonged Closure is a Security Threat," *Hatzofeh* (in Hebrew), September 16, 1998, p. 7.

31 Cabinet Communiqué, July 12, 1998, communicated by the Cabinet Secretariat, released by the Israeli Foreign Ministry, online at http://www.israel-mfa.gov.il/.

32 Hassan Asfour interview, "West Bank and Gaza Strip: PA Official on Situation in Territories," *Cairo Voice of the Arabs*, September 14, 1998, in FBIS-NES-98-257, September 14, 1998.

33 Huberman, "A Prolonged Closure is a Security Threat."

34 Ibid.

35 Lee Hockstader, "For Palestinian Residents of Gaza, 5 Years of Peace Bear Bitter Fruit," *Washington Post*, September 14, 1998, p. A14.

36 David Makovsky and News Agencies, "Peace Talks Stuck on 'Safe Passage' Routes," *Ha'aretz* (English internet edition), September 15, 1998.

37 "The Wye River Memorandum," October 23, 1998, available on the Israeli Ministry of Foreign Affairs web site at http://www.israel.org/mfa/go.asp?MFAH07o10/.

38 Israelis wanted to name the airport after Dahiniya, a nearby village controlled by Israel and home to the families of seven Palestinians who collaborated with Israel and are regarded by Palestinians as traitors. Palestinians were offended by this idea and insisted on naming the airport for Gaza. See Miral Fahmy, "Gaza Airport Hostage to Mideast Deadlock," *Reuters*, March 27, 1998, and Doug Struck, "Disputes Clipping Airport's Opening," *Washington Post*, March 28, 1998, p. A17. Palestinians were also much more eager than Israelis to have the word "international" as part of the airport's name.

39 Yasir Abd Rabbuh, interviewed on *Voice of Palestine*, Ramallah, "Palestinian Information Minister Says USA Being Two-faced in Negotiations," October 26, 1997, published in *BBC Summary of World Broadcasts*, October 28, 1997.

40 Deborah Sontag, "Palestinians Walking on Air at Opening of Gaza Airport," *New York Times*, November 25, 1998, p. 1.

Chapter 6

Conclusions

The U.S. experience in seeking to use economic initiatives to foster the Arab–Israeli peace process offers a number of lessons. It is worthwhile to contemplate these lessons, given that the peace process, for better or for worse, will probably continue for a long time to come.

One basic fact stands out above all else: In the Middle East, politics comes before business, but business can help to reinforce politics. Although economic efforts will rarely be enough of a force to pave a path from hostility to peace, they can be useful in supporting and cementing progress along that path. When the basic elements of a peace agreement are already in place, the process of reaching that agreement has usually involved each side making difficult compromises to the other. In such situations, economic incentives can help to clinch the deal by assisting both parties in winning domestic approval for the compromises. Furthermore, once political arrangements are agreed upon, economic efforts can play a role in expanding the peace to involve the populations, as opposed to simply the leaders. If financial incentives are given a larger mandate than this—for example, if large amounts of aid are offered to entice governments to make a deal regardless of how far apart they are on political issues, or if initiatives implicitly promise populations immediate and substantial peace dividends—they not only are unlikely to be of help, but they may indeed play a negative role in the progress toward peace.

The primary reason why some economic initiatives can actually be destructive is the danger of unfulfilled expectations. This risk also indicates several other lessons. Whereas it is important to avoid making unrealistic promises with regard to economic initiatives, it is equally vital to make every effort to follow through on commitments once they are made.

The desired political and economic results of these endeavors are often far less immediate than either the United States or the regional parties would hope. Ultimate success requires persistence, and leaders should also keep the promises modest at the outset. In other words, aim low, but be sure to deliver. The temptation to make grand promises and predictions to sell a government or a population on a deal it would otherwise reject is unwise, because the almost inevitable disappointment to follow will sour people on both the failed economic initiative and the peace agreement. The wave of enthusiasm that swept Gaza after the Oslo Declaration of Principles was based in part on the expectation that prosperity was around the corner, when in fact there was ample reason to expect from the beginning that the economic advantages would come slowly and only if the peace process was reinforced. Experience from country after country around the world has showed that international aid can do only so much. Rebuilding Europe after World War II took most of a decade; not even the Marshall Plan worked a miracle in one year.

Perhaps, under the best political circumstances, economic efforts could provide their own momentum. When the diplomatic atmosphere is problematic, however, as it has certainly been in this case, initiatives require sustained efforts and dedication at the highest levels. The lesson is to make sure to stay on target. Builders for Peace failed for a complex combination of reasons, but certainly one of them was the fact that, after a high-profile beginning with President Bill Clinton and Vice President Al Gore, the project received no sustained attention from the upper echelons of U.S. policymaking. The multilateral track of the peace process also suffered from an insufficient level of attention paid by the key U.S. figures who may have had the influence and clout to sustain it in the face of adversity.

Part of the reason that expectations may be unfulfilled is that sometimes the impression is given that an economic initiative will make a quick difference, when in fact most of the initiatives take years to become fully effective. The lesson is to indicate a realistic time frame for results. MENA summits, as an example, may have played a useful role in facilitating people-to-people contacts among Arabs and Israelis. They may also have served the purpose of introducing outside investors to a region they might otherwise have easily overlooked; all of this, in turn, ultimately contributed to political support for peace by giving businesspeople a sense that it can bring increased prosperity for all. Yet, these results are more long-term than immediate, especially for all but the most wealthy business elites from each country. The vigorous promotion that brought regional players, and particularly Arabs, to these summits resulted in a growing sense of disappointment as the contacts made and deals presented did not lead to notice-able, immediate gains in wealth for the populations involved. Admittedly, modest promises of a slow, long-term process of building a foundation for prosperity would make a much less appealing sales pitch, but these prom-ises would be much easier to fulfill and much less likely to provoke a backlash of disappointment.

The policy speeches that announce or encourage new plans would do well to temper projections for increased prosperity and cooperation by pointing out the inherent limitations and probable delays of rewards from any such effort. U.S. leaders have an even more direct responsibility to avoid making promises on behalf of their own country that they may not have the authority to fulfill. The nature of the American system of democ-racy dictates that commitments on the part of administration officials, to the extent that they require an appropriation of funds, are conditioned upon congressional approval. Given the reluctance of Congress to spend addi-tional money on foreign aid in general and on the Middle East in particu-lar, administration officials need to impress upon regional players the tenuous nature of any financial commitment unless and until a clear com-mitment from Congress is obtained on a specific project. In other words, they should promise only that which can be delivered. A case in point is the MENABANK, as the administration publicly backed the establishment of the bank and encouraged other countries to sign on, only to find that Congress would not fund the U.S. share. Whether the bank was a sensible project to initiate, the prominent role played in the planning stages made Washington's subsequent failure to provide its opening share detrimental to U.S. credibility. This illustrates not only the vital importance of timely consultation and coordination among various branches and agencies of the U.S. government, but also the necessity of U.S. officials making only modest pledges that they can be assured of fulfilling. Both the administration and Congress should keep in mind the need to consult early and regularly, for U.S. credibility is damaged when an administration breaks its promise because of a lack of coordination between the two branches.

It may be tempting to assume that all but a few extremists accept the economic advantages of doing business together. Yet, not everyone in the Middle East is sold on the benefits of free markets; the forces of old-fash-ioned protectionism and narrow economic nationalism are powerful ev-erywhere, in Israel as well as in Arab states. Moreover, many throughout the Levant firmly believe that if the other side is more prosperous, it will be a more powerful opponent rather than a more likely peace partner. At the level of the officials who must inspect the goods and process the paperwork, there is still a widespread attitude that what is good for Arabs is bad for Israelis and vice-versa. In other words, U.S. officials should expect opposition to economic cooperation. It was no aberration when fears were expressed at the Amman MENA summit that economic cooperation is an updated version of Israel's long-standing plans to dominate the region.

Especially in light of the limitations on what the United States will be prepared to provide, it is particularly important to set priorities about what counts the most. The natural impulse of the officials administering economic initiatives is to target the same goals they have been aiming for in other countries, which means economic objectives like helping the poorest, combating corruption, and concentrating government investment funds on projects with a high rate of return, as well, perhaps, as political goals like good governance and promoting civil society. These objectives are all worthwhile aims, but they are not necessarily the most important items for the peace process. It may be more appropriate to give a lower priority to some of those objectives and to assign a higher priority to peace process problems, like increasing the effectiveness of the Palestinian Security Services' counterterrorism efforts. Furthermore, it may be worthwhile to tie aid disbursement to Palestinian progress on specific peace process issues. Much as U.S. aid in some Latin American countries ties cash payments to the eradication of coca plants (so many hectares torn up means so many million of dollars released), so too could cash tranches be tied to progress on difficult issues like registering otherwise-illegal Palestinian weapons. Not only can such cash tranches create an incentive for the PA to carry out difficult measures, but they can provide the authorities an explanation to offer the populace about why the measures must be done—and these measures can have a substantial economic impact, by preventing terrorism and therefore limiting the closures that have so hit the PA economy.

Although it is true that finance alone cannot work political miracles, it is also true that most economic endeavors can be politically effective only if they adhere to basic principles of business; while some Israelis have shown a willingness to enter into joint projects that are not sound business ideas for the sake of peace, most of their Arab counterparts do not share the luxury or the proclivity to do so. Similarly, investors from outside the region may be persuaded to look into business opportunities in the Middle East out of a desire to support peace, but they will not actually invest unless the project and the investment climate represent a reasonable business prospect, without undue risk. The best examples of Arab–Israeli economic cooperation are cases of businesspeople who are willing to take the political step of dealing with each other, but who also see a good opportunity to make a profit. Businesspeople like Omar Salah of Jordan and Dov Lautman of Israel are committed to the peace process, but they are also all committed to being successful entrepreneurs. The joint ventures in which they are involved are succeeding not only because of the rare willingness of those individuals to break taboos, but also because they follow the basic logic of business; they are providing basic necessities like textiles of good quality, and at competitive prices. The employees of these operations do not necesarily choose to work for them out of support for the peace process, but rather because of more typical ambitions—they cite good working conditions, competitive wages, and excellent benefits. Many do come to have altered views of the peace process and their former foes, but this is a desirable side effect that becomes possible only because of sound business foundations.

It would seem logical that the political impact of economic efforts would be greatest when those efforts are well publicized, so the relevant populations know who has been responsible. Yet, some of the most politically effective efforts of U.S. officials occur away from the public limelight. For example, although U.S. officials have received almost no publicity and only limited success, their efforts to mitigate the damage of closures and other Israeli restrictions on the Palestinian economy have served the invaluable political purpose of improving Arab officials' image of America; whereas once they saw U.S. officials as siding automatically with Israel, now they see America more as an objective partner who cares about them as well as Israel. It is therefore particularly beneficial for the peace process when U.S. officials can act on behalf of Arab friends without jeopardizing basic Israeli interests or the U.S.–Israeli relationship. These efforts, which occur on a daily basis at border crossings and elsewhere, may lack the glory and glitter of a large international gathering of high-level politicians, but they offer political credibility for the United States that can be useful at sensitive political junctures.

In sum, U.S. economic efforts to foster advancements in the peace process have generally been worthwhile, but they can be modified to correct past errors and to avoid potential future pitfalls. U.S. economic initiatives have helped to promote people-to-people contacts, to sell difficult compromises to hesitant populations, and to remind regional leaders that political and economic stability can help to attract outside investment. By minimizing unrealistic expectations, maintaining a consistent level of commitment, and coordinating among different branches and agencies, U.S. officials can maximize the benefits their economic initiatives bring to the peace process.

Recent Books

from The Washington Institute

NEW MEDIA, NEW POLITICS?
From Satellite Television to the Internet in the Arab World
Jon B. Alterman

Describes the new forms of the Arab media—including international Arabic newspapers and magazines, Arabic satellite TV services, and the internet—and analyzes their present and future political consequences for national and regional developments. *November 1998, 80 pp., ISBN 0-944029-28-0*

IRAN UNDER KHATAMI
A Political, Economic, and Military Assessment
Patrick Clawson, Michael Eisenstadt, Eliyahu Kanovsky, David Menashri

In an update of the Institute's best-selling Focus on Iran series, the authors analyze the changes in Iranian government policies in the year since Muhammad Khatami became president. Each chapter updates the author's previous book to create a comprehensive view of Iran's military, economy, and domestic politics. Includes an additional analysis of U.S. policies toward Iran, focusing on if—and how—these policies should change. *October 1998, 112 pp., ISBN 0-944029-27-2*

BUILDING TOWARD CRISIS
Saddam Husayn's Strategy for Survival
Amatzia Baram

U.S. Institute of Peace Scholar Amatzia Baram examines the domestic coalition supporting Saddam Husayn and techniques the Iraqi president uses to maintain that coalition. While providing an extensive look at Saddam's family tree and the importance of relations in understanding Saddam's power base, this book explains how the Iraqi president has used the international community to influence his domestic standing and to garner needed support in the Arab world. *Policy Paper no. 47, July 1998, 156 pp., ISBN 0-944029-25-6*

IRAQ STRATEGY REVIEW
Options for U.S. Policy
Patrick L. Clawson, editor

Seven years after the Gulf War, Saddam Husayn is still in power in Baghdad and still a thorn in America's side. Meanwhile, U.S. policy toward Iraq is under fire from critics both foreign and domestic. By presenting essays by six Middle East scholars that assess Washington's potential courses of action, *Iraq Strategy Review* offers a means of analyzing America's options regarding the Iraqi dictator. This book is an invaluable tool for U.S policymakers and others interested in America's Iraq policy. It provides the crucial starting point for public debate over how the United States should handle Saddam's Iraq. *July 1998, 180 pp., ISBN 0-944029-26-4*

'KNIVES, TANKS, AND MISSILES'
Israel's Security Revolution
Eliot Cohen, Michael Eisenstadt, Andrew Bacevich

While the day's headlines focus on the stalemate in the Arab–Israeli peace process, the necessity of deterring and—potentially—fighting war remains the supreme challenge for Israel's leaders. Complicating this effort is the remarkable pace of technological change that has created what experts term a "revolution in military affairs." Weapons are "smarter" and more lethal than ever before, terrorism can now pose a strategic threat, and missiles can now bring an enemy thousands of miles away to a nation's borders. To understand the answers Israeli military planners and strategic thinkers have given to these critical questions—so as to glean appropriate lessons for the U.S. armed forces—these three military scholars, at the request of the Pentagon's Office of Net Assessment, undertook this special study of Israel's security revolution. *June 1998, 156 pp., ISBN 0-944029-72-8*

JERUSALEM'S HOLY PLACES AND THE PEACE PROCESS
Marshall J. Breger and Thomas A. Idinopulos

Analyzes more than four hundred years of Jerusalem's history to glean practical, operational lessons from Ottoman, British, Jordanian, and Israeli control of the city and its holy sites: what does and does not work. With the May 1999 deadline for the expiration of the Oslo Accords looming, this study offers a useful guide to shaping a future for Jerusalem based on peace, openness, civility, and tolerance. *Policy Paper no. 46, May 1998, 76 pp., ISBN 0-944029-73-6*

For a complete list of all Institute publications, go online at
www.washingtoninstitute.org

DATE DUE

5/3/11		

Brodart Co.   Cat. # 55 137 001   Printed in USA